PRACTICAL JAPANESE 2

JLPT N4 Grammar and Useful Expressions
JLPT N4レベルの基礎文法と使える表現

小川 清美＝著
Orrin Cummins＝英語監修

IBC
IBCパブリッシング

はじめに

本書は2016年に出版されたPRACTICAL JAPANESEの続編で、さらに日本語を文法から学びたい人のための本です。

PRACTICAL JAPANESEは、日本に短期間滞在する人が、手っ取り早く必要なフレーズを基本的な文法を理解しながら覚えられるように作りました。本書では、文法に重点をおき、単なる丸覚えではなく応用ができることを目標に作りました。

また、文法以外にも、日本人が会話の中でよく使う表現「とにかく」「ところで」なども紹介してあります。

もう一つの本書の特徴は、外国人学習者からよく聞かれる、似ている表現の違いをWhat's the difference? として取り上げていることです。これは、日々のレッスンでよく聞かれる質問や、生徒がよくする間違いをもとにしてありますので、きっと皆さんの疑問にも役に立つのではないかと思います。

PRACTICAL JAPANESEと、このPRACTICAL JAPANESE ２とで、JLPT（日本語能力試験）のN4レベルの文法を約70％学ぶこともできますので、JLPT対策としても活用いただけると思います。

多くの人が本書を使って楽しく日本語を学べることを願っております。

最後に、ご尽力いただいたIBCパブリッシングの皆様と日本語教師としてアドバイスをくださった片野聡子さん、そして編集だけでなく外国人としての視点で本書を書くことに協力してくれた夫に感謝いたします。

小川 清美

Preface

This book is a continuation of *Practical Japanese* (2016) and is intended for those who wish to delve deeper into Japanese from a grammatical point of view.

I wrote the previous book so that people who found themselves residing in Japan for a brief time could expediently learn necessary phrases while gaining a basic understanding of Japanese grammar. My goal with this book is to help learners transition beyond rote memorization by focusing on the application of important grammatical concepts. Several new expressions used by Japanese natives in conversation, such as とにかく and ところで, are also introduced within these pages.

Another feature of this book is its "What's the difference?" sections that focus on the practical differences between expressions whose close similarity can pose problems for foreign learners of the language. These are expressions that students often ask about in lessons and tend to make mistakes with, so I believe that examining them in more detail will be helpful.

Since *Practical Japanese* and *Practical Japanese 2* collectively cover about 70% of the grammar that appears on the N4 level of the Japanese Language Proficiency Test, they can also be used as JLPT preparation materials.
I hope that this book helps everyone learn some Japanese in a fun and enjoyable manner.

Finally, I would like to extend my heartfelt gratitude to everyone at IBC Publishing for their tireless efforts in making this book a reality; to Satoko Katano for her advice as a fellow Japanese language teacher; and to my husband who not only edited this book but provided valuable insight from the perspective of a foreign learner of the language.

Kiyomi Ogawa

Contents

How to Use This Book

This book is intended for those who are already familiar with the basic grammar introduced in *Practical Japanese 1*.

Those grammar topics are briefly reviewed at the start of each chapter. Be sure that you understand them before diving into the new grammar.

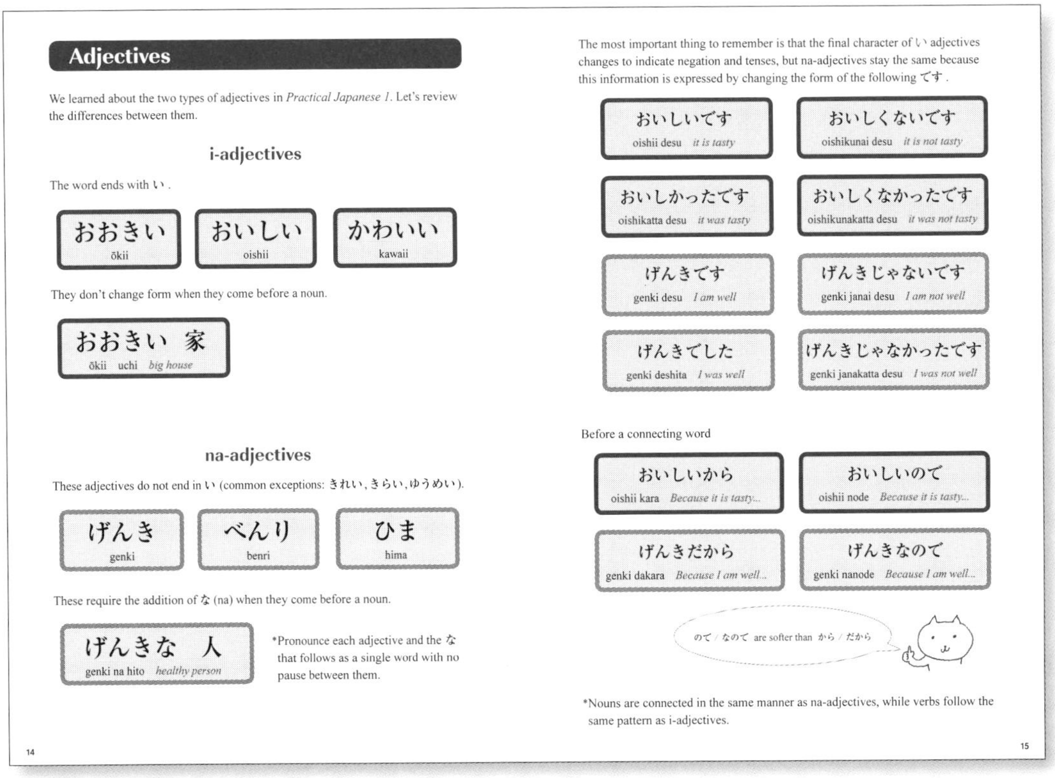

Adjectives

We learned about the two types of adjectives in *Practical Japanese 1*. Let's review the differences between them.

i-adjectives

The word ends with い.

おおきい ōkii

おいしい oishii

かわいい kawaii

They don't change form when they come before a noun.

おおきい 家 ōkii uchi *big house*

na-adjectives

These adjectives do not end in い (common exceptions: きれい, きらい, ゆうめい).

げんき genki

べんり benri

ひま hima

These require the addition of な (na) when they come before a noun.

げんきな 人 genki na hito *healthy person*

*Pronounce each adjective and the な that follows as a single word with no pause between them.

14

The most important thing to remember is that the final character of い adjectives changes to indicate negation and tenses, but na-adjectives stay the same because this information is expressed by changing the form of the following です.

おいしいです oishii desu *it is tasty*

おいしくないです oishikunai desu *it is not tasty*

おいしかったです oishikatta desu *it was tasty*

おいしくなかったです oishikunakatta desu *it was not tasty*

げんきです genki desu *I am well*

げんきじゃないです genki janai desu *I am not well*

げんきでした genki deshita *I was well*

げんきじゃなかったです genki janakatta desu *I was not well*

Before a connecting word

おいしいから oishii kara *Because it is tasty...*

おいしいので oishii node *Because it is tasty...*

げんきだから genki dakara *Because I am well...*

げんきなので genki nanode *Because I am well...*

*Nouns are connected in the same manner as na-adjectives, while verbs follow the same pattern as i-adjectives.

15

On each lesson page, you will learn a new grammar pattern and the rules for using it.

Several styles are introduced to prepare you for conversing at different politeness levels.

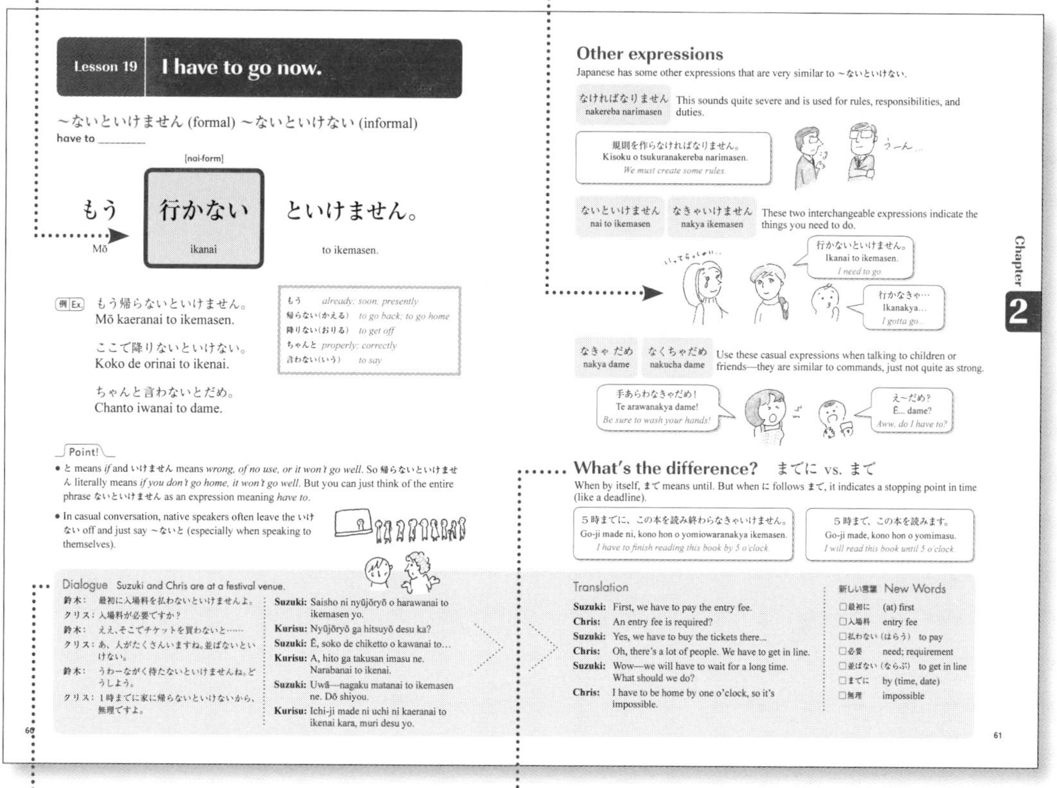

Lesson 19 **I have to go now.**

~ないといけません (formal) ~ないといけない (informal)
have to ________

もう [nai-form] 行かない といけません。
Mō ikanai to ikemasen.

例 Ex. もう帰らないといけません。
Mō kaeranai to ikemasen.

ここで降りないといけない。
Koko de orinai to ikenai.

ちゃんと言わないとだめ。
Chanto iwanai to dame.

もう	*already; soon; presently*
帰らない(かえる)	*to go back; to go home*
降りない(おりる)	*to get off*
ちゃんと	*properly; correctly*
言わない(いう)	*to say*

Point!

- と means *if* and いけません means *wrong, of no use, or it won't go well*. So 帰らないといけません literally means *if you don't go home, it won't go well*. But you can just think of the entire phrase ないといけません as an expression meaning *have to*.
- In casual conversation, native speakers often leave the いけない off and just say ~ないと (especially when speaking to themselves).

Dialogue Suzuki and Chris are at a festival venue.

鈴木：最初に入場料を払わないといけませんよ。
クリス：入場料が必要ですか？
鈴木：ええ、そこでチケットを買わないと……
クリス：あ、人がたくさんいますね。並ばないといけない。
鈴木：うわーながく待たないといけませんね。どうしよう。
クリス：1時までに家に帰らないといけないから、無理ですよ。

Suzuki: Saisho ni nyūjōryō o harawanai to ikemasen yo.
Kurisu: Nyūjōryō ga hitsuyō desu ka?
Suzuki: Ē, soko de chiketto o kawanai to…
Kurisu: A, hito ga takusan imasu ne. Narabanai to ikenai.
Suzuki: Uwā—nagaku matanai to ikemasen ne. Dō shiyou.
Kurisu: Ichi-ji made ni uchi ni kaeranai to ikenai kara, muri desu yo.

60

Other expressions

Japanese has some other expressions that are very similar to ~ないといけない.

なければなりません nakereba narimasen — This sounds quite severe and is used for rules, responsibilities, and duties.

規則を作らなければなりません。
Kisoku o tsukuranakereba narimasen.
We must create some rules.

うーん…

ないといけません nai to ikemasen / なきゃいけません nakya ikemasen — These two interchangeable expressions indicate the things you need to do.

行かないといけません。
Ikanai to ikemasen.
I need to go.

行かなきゃ…
Ikanakya…
I gotta go…

なきゃ だめ nakya dame / なくちゃだめ nakucha dame — Use these casual expressions when talking to children or friends—they are similar to commands, just not quite as strong.

手あらわなきゃだめ！
Te arawanakya dame!
Be sure to wash your hands!

え~だめ？
Ē... dame?
Aww, do I have to?

What's the difference? までに vs. まで

When by itself, まで means until. But when に follows まで, it indicates a stopping point in time (like a deadline).

5時までに、この本を読み終わらなきゃいけません。
Go-ji made ni, kono hon o yomiowaranakya ikemasen.
I have to finish reading this book by 5 o'clock.

5時まで、この本を読みます。
Go-ji made, kono hon o yomimasu.
I will read this book until 5 o'clock.

Translation

Suzuki: First, we have to pay the entry fee.
Chris: An entry fee is required?
Suzuki: Yes, we have to buy the tickets there...
Chris: Oh, there's a lot of people. We have to get in line.
Suzuki: Wow—we will have to wait for a long time. What should we do?
Chris: I have to be home by one o'clock, so it's impossible.

新しい言葉 New Words

□最初に	(at) first
□入場料	entry fee
□払わない (はらう)	to pay
□必要	need; requirement
□並ばない (ならぶ)	to get in line
□までに	by (time, date)
□無理	impossible

Chapter 2

61

The "What's the difference?" sections explain the distinction between similar expressions in more detail.

After learning each grammar pattern, read the corresponding dialogue to get a sense of how the pattern is used in a natural setting.

Useful Expressions

お久しぶりです
o-hisashiburi desu
it's been a long time

ひさしぶり
hisashiburi
long time no see

ところで
tokorode
by the way

そういえば
sō ieba
speaking of that

やっぱり
yappari
as I thought

さすがですね
sasuga desu ne
I'd expect nothing less

とにかく
tonikaku
anyway

もう
mō
already; more

もう１２時です
mō jūni-ji desu
it is already twelve o'clock

もう１回
mō ikkai
one more time

もうちょっと
mō chotto
a little more

まだ
mada
still; yet

まだ考えています
mada kangaete imasu
I'm still thinking

まだ終わりません
mada owarimasen
not finished yet

おめでとう（ございます）
omedetō (gozaimasu)
congratulations

おかげさまで
o-kagesama de
thanks to you

誕生日おめでとう（ございます）
tanjōbi omedetō (gozaimasu)
happy birthday

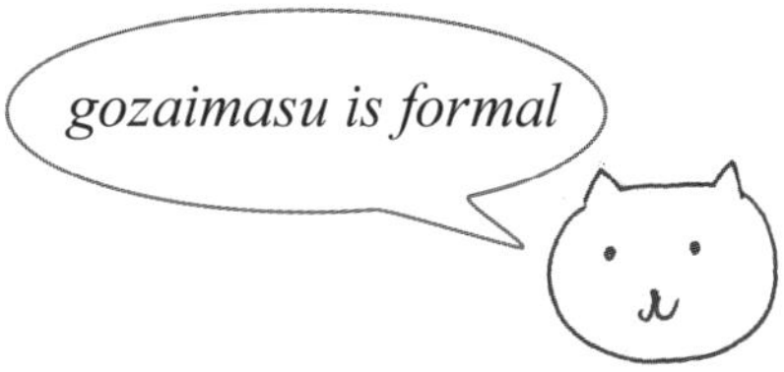

おなかがすきました
onaka ga sukimashita
I'm hungry

おなかすいた（casual）
onaka suita
I'm hungry

のどがかわきました
nodo ga kawakimashita
I'm thirsty

のどかわいた（casual）
nodo kawaita
I'm thirsty

場合によります
baai ni yorimasu
it depends on the situation

*Other words can replace 場合 to say *it depends on something else*, but よります can't be used by itself.

場所によります
basho ni yorimasu
depends on the place

人によります
hito ni yorimasu
depends on the person

一括でよろしいですか？
ikkatsu de yoroshii desuka?
Will you be paying in full now?

*Cashiers might ask this if you pay with a credit card – even if your total is only 100 yen or so!

Basic Sentence Structure

subject		noun/adjective	
私	は	日本人	です。
watashi	wa	nihonjin	desu.

question word		noun/adjective	
なに・だれ・どれ・どこ・いつ	が	いい	ですか？
nani · dare · dore · doko · itsu	ga	ii	desu ka?

subject		noun		adjective	
私	は	日本	が	好き	です。
watashi	wa	Nihon	ga	suki	desu.

subject		object		verb
私	は	日本語	を	勉強します。
watashi	wa	nihongo	o	benkyō shimasu.

subject		place		verb
私	は	日本	に	行きます。
watashi	wa	Nihon	ni	ikimasu.

subject		place		person		verb
私	は	日本	に	友達	と	行きます。
watashi	wa	Nihon	ni	tomodachi		ikimasu.

subject		place		vehicle		verb
私	は	東京	に	電車	で	行きます。
watashi	wa	Tōkyō	ni	densha	de	ikimasu.

place		inanimate object		verb
京都	に	お寺	が	あります。
Kyōto	ni	otera	ga	arimasu.

place		animate object		verb
京都	に	友達	が	います。
Kyōto	ni	tomodachi	ga	imasu.

Particle Usage

X	from	Y	to
place/time		place/time	
東京/10時 Tōkyō / jū-ji	から	京都/8時 Kyōto / hachi-ji	まで

X	and	Y
noun		noun
東京 Tōkyō	と	京都 Kyōto

X	and	Y	etc.
noun		noun	
名古屋 Nagoya	とか	大阪 Ōsaka	とか

(formal)

X	and	Y	etc.
noun		noun	
名古屋 Nagoya	や	大阪 Ōsaka	など

Day/Time	
月曜日/1時	に
getsuyōbi / ichi-ji	ni

Chapter 1

Nouns and Adjectives

第1章　名詞と形容詞

Adjectives

We learned about the two types of adjectives in *Practical Japanese 1*. Let's review the differences between them.

i-adjectives

The word ends with い.

おおきい	おいしい	かわいい
ōkii	oishii	kawaii

They don't change form when they come before a noun.

おおきい　家
ōkii　uchi　*big house*

na-adjectives

These adjectives do not end in い (common exceptions: きれい, きらい, ゆうめい).

げんき	べんり	ひま
genki	benri	hima

These require the addition of な (na) when they come before a noun.

げんきな　人
genki na hito　*healthy person*

*Pronounce each adjective and the な that follows as a single word with no pause between them.

The most important thing to remember is that the final character of i-adjectives changes to indicate negation and tenses, but na-adjectives stay the same because this information is expressed by changing the form of the following です .

おいしいです oishii desu *it is tasty*	おいしくないです oishikunai desu *it is not tasty*
おいしかったです oishikatta desu *it was tasty*	おいしくなかったです oishikunakatta desu *it was not tasty*
げんきです genki desu *I am well*	げんきじゃないです genki janai desu *I am not well*
げんきでした genki deshita *I was well*	げんきじゃなかったです genki janakatta desu *I was not well*

Before a connecting word

おいしいから oishii kara *Because it is tasty...*	おいしいので oishii node *Because it is tasty...*
げんきだから genki dakara *Because I am well...*	げんきなので genki nanode *Because I am well...*

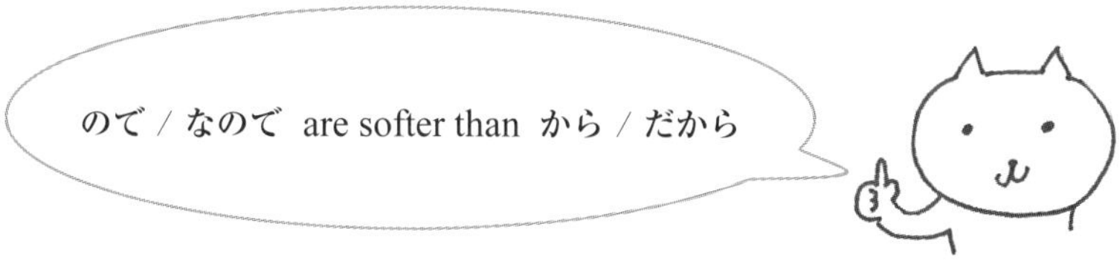

*Nouns are connected in the same manner as na-adjectives, while verbs follow the same pattern as i-adjectives.

Lesson 1 That big white building is the post office.

	[adjective]	[adjective]	
あの	大きくて	白い	ビルが郵便局です。
Ano	ōkikute	shiroi	biru ga yūbinkyoku desu.

例 Ex. うちのネコは小さくて黒いです。
Uchi no neko wa chīsakute kuroi desu.

安くて軽いバッグが欲しいです。
Yasukute karui baggu ga hoshii desu.

京都は伝統的で古い街です。
Kyōto wa dentōteki de furui machi desu.

大きくて（おおきい）*big and*
小さくて（ちいさい）*small and*
安くて（やすい）*cheap and*
軽い *light*
ほしい *want*
伝統的で *traditional and*
古い *old*

Point!

- Multiple descriptive words are linked according to their type of speech.
- i-adjectives: change the い to くて　　小さい → 小さくて
- na-adjectives and noun: add で　　伝統的 → 伝統的で

Some adjectives can become nouns according to the rules below.

Colors	白い	→ 白
i-adjectives	大きい	→ 大きさ
na-adjectives	きれい	→ きれいさ

Dialogue

ミカ：ちいさくて、茶色くて、かわいくて、ナッツをよく食べます。何の動物でしょう。
ジョン：もしかして、リスですか？
ミカ：はい、そうです。じゃ、次。
白くて耳が長くて目が赤いです。
ジョン：うさぎです。

Mika: Chīsakute, chairokute, kawaikute, nattsu o yoku tabemasu. Nan no dōbutsu deshō?
Jon: Moshikashite, risu desu ka?
Mika: Hai, sō desu. Ja, tsugi.
Shirokute mimi ga nagakute me ga akai desu.
Jon: Usagi desu.

大きさ ōkisa *size*

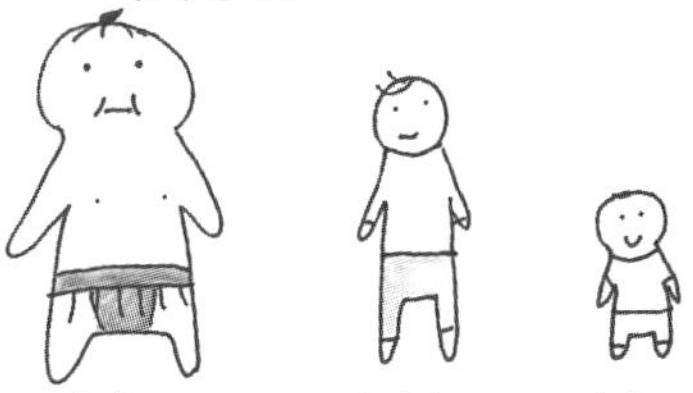

大きい
ōkii

中くらい
chūkurai

小さい
chīsai

重さ omosa *weight*

重い
omoi

軽い
karui

形 katachi *shape*

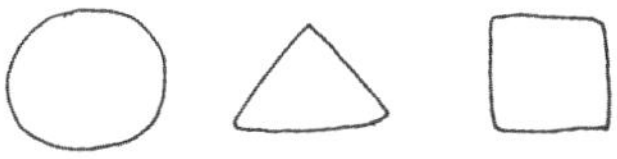

まる
maru

さんかく
sankaku

しかく
shikaku

長さ nagasa *length*

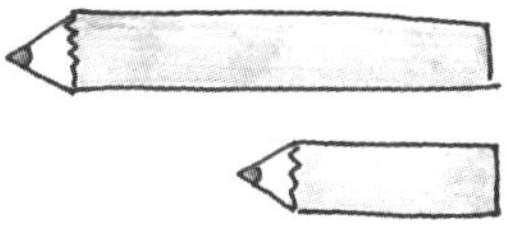

長い
nagai

短い
mijikai

高さ takasa *height*

背が高い
se ga takai

背が低い
se ga hikui

感触 kanshoku *texture*

やわらかい
yawarakai

かたい
katai

肌触りがいい
hadazawari ga ii
(used for cloth)

onomatopoeia (*connect with* で)

ピカピカ
pikapika

ふわふわ
fuwafuwa

ぐちゃぐちゃ
guchagucha

Translation

Mika: It is small, brown, cute and eats lots of nuts. What animal is it?

John: Could it be a squirrel?

Mika: Yes, correct. OK, next one.
It is white with long ears and red eyes.

John: It's a rabbit.

新しい言葉 New Words

- ☐茶色くて(ちゃいろ) brown
- ☐ナッツ nuts
- ☐もしかして Could it be...?
- ☐リス squirrel
- ☐次 next
- ☐うさぎ rabbit

Lesson 2

She is pretty and kind, so everyone likes her.

[adjective] [adjective]

彼女は **かわいい** し **親切** だし、みんな彼女が好きです。

Kanojo wa **kawaii** shi **shinsetsu** dashi, minna kanojo ga suki desu.

例 Ex. 日本はきれいだし、人が親切だし…(好きです。)
Nihon wa kirei dashi, hito ga shinsetsu dashi...(suki desu.)

このバッグは大きいし、値段も手ごろだし、いいですよ。
Kono baggu wa ōkii shi, nedan mo tegoro dashi, ii desu yo.

あの人はこわいし乱暴だし、苦手です。
Ano hito wa kowai shi ranbō dashi, nigate desu.

し・だし *and, also*
値段 *price (of a product)*
手ごろ *reasonable*
乱暴 *rough*
苦手 *don't get along with*

Point!

- To connect descriptive words that describe reasons or emotions, use し and だし (see next page).
- i-adjectives: し → かわいいし
- Nouns and na-adjectives: だし → 親切だし

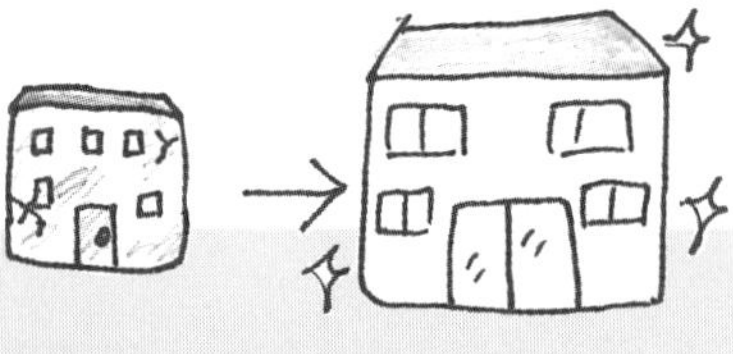

Dialogue

レナード：	今のアパートは、小さいし古いし不便なので、新しくて広いところに引っ越したいです。
不動産屋：	このアパートはどうですか？
レナード：	ああ、いいですね。駅が近いし。家賃はいくらですか？
不動産屋：	管理費込みで6万です。

Renādo:	Ima no apāto wa, chīsai shi furui shi fuben nanode, atarashikute hiroi tokoro ni hikkoshitai desu.
Fudōsanya:	Kono apāto wa dō desu ka?
Renādo:	Ā, ii desu ne. Eki ga chikai shi. Yachin wa ikura desu ka?
Fudōsanya:	Kanrihi komi de roku-man en desu.

What's the difference? くて・で vs. し・だし

し and だし are used to connect multiple reasons, but you can also say a single reason if you can't think of what to say next or if you are hesitant to say more—the use of し・だし implies that you have other, unstated reasons.

Chapter 1

くて・で

マイクさんはどの人ですか？
Maiku-san wa dono hito desu ka?
Which person is Mike?

背が高くて、髪が短い人ですよ。
Se ga takakute, kami ga mijikai hito desu.
He's the tall one with short hair.

し・だし

どうしてマイクさんが好きですか？
Dōshite Maiku-san ga suki desu ka?
Why do you like Mike?

やさしいし、イケメンだし…
Yasashii shi, ikemen dashi...
He's sweet and cool....

One more thing!
These expressions can also be used after verbs.

飲みに行きましょう！
Nomi ni ikimashō!
Let's go drinking!

病院に行きますし…すみません。
Byōin ni ikimasu shi... sumimasen.
I'm heading to the hospital...sorry.

いいね！
Ii ne!
Sounds great!

ケーキが食べられるし、ジュースも飲めるし！
Kēki ga taberareru shi, jūsu mo nomeru shi!
We can eat cake and drink some juice!

Translation

Lenard: My current apartment is small, old and inconvenient, so I want to move to a new and spacious place.

Agent: How about this apartment?

Lenard: Oh, this is good. It's close to the station. How much is the rent?

Agent: Including the management fee, it is sixty thousand yen.

新しい言葉 New Words

- □不動産屋　real estate agency
- □広い　spacious
- □引っ越したい（ひっこす）　want to move
- □家賃　rent
- □管理費　management fee
- □込み　included

Lesson 3 This train is faster than that train.

[topic A]		[topic B]		[adjective]	
この電車	のほうが	あの電車	より	速い	です。
Kono densha	no hō ga	ano densha	yori	hayai	desu.

例 Ex. ジョンさんのほうがマイクさんより背が高いです。
Jon-san no hō ga Maiku-san yori se ga takai desu.

テレビよりネット動画のほうが好きです。
Terebi yori netto dōga no hō ga suki desu.

コーヒーとお茶、どちら(どっち)がいいですか？
Kōhī to ocha, dochira (docchi) ga ii desu ka?

ほう	*way*
より	*than*
ネット動画	*online video*
どちら	*which (formal)*
どっち	*which (casual)*

Point!

- Put のほうが and より after the nouns being compared. The adjective comes at the end and does not change form.
- AのほうがBより adjective → *A is more (adjective) than*
- のほう is sometimes omitted : AとBどちら (のほう) がいいですか？
  → *Which is better, A or B?*
- のほうが is pronounced as a single word.

Dialogue At the food court

西岡： うどんとラーメン、どっちがいいですか？
マイク： そうですね…うどんのほうがいいです。
西岡： すみません、うどん二つおねがいします。
店員： はい、うどんがお二つですね。あたたかいのと冷たいのがございますが。
マイク： あったかいのお願いします。

Nishioka: Udon to rāmen, docchi ga ii desu ka?
Maiku: Sō desu ne…udon no hō ga ii desu.
Nishioka: Sumimasen, udon futatsu onegai shimasu.
Tenin: Hai, udon ga o-futatsu desu ne. Atatakai no to tsumetai no ga gozaimasu ga.
Maiku: Attakai no onegai shimasu.

A is (more) ______ than B　AのほうがBより〜〜です

Consider the following two sentences:

コーヒーのほうがお茶より好きです。 Kōhī no hō ga ocha yori suki desu. *I like coffee more than tea.*	お茶よりコーヒーのほうが好きです。 Ocha yori kōhī no hō ga suki desu. *I like tea less than coffee.*

Both of these sentences are correct and basically say the same thing, but sticking to one format or the other can keep you from getting confused.

Both / Either

どちら(どっち)も好きです。 Dochira (docchi) mo suki desu. *I like both of them.*	どちら(どっち)も好きじゃないです。 Dochira (docchi) mo suki janai desu. *I don't like either of them.*

What's the difference?　ほう vs. もっと

The nuance here is that you like both of them but you like cats more.

犬が好きだけど、ネコはもっと好きです。 Inu ga suki da kedo, neko wa motto suki desu. *I like dogs, but I like cats more.*	日本語がもっと上手になりたいです。 Nihongo ga motto jōzu ni naritai desu. *I want to get even better at Japanese.*

ほうが can't be used for the above statements because they aren't comparisons between two things.

× → 日本語のほうが上手になりたい。

◯ → 日本語のほうが英語より上手です。

*〜になる(see page 26)

Translation

Nishioka: Which do you prefer, udon or ramen?

Mike: Hmm...I prefer udon.

Nishioka: Excuse me, two orders of udon please.

Employee: Okay, two udon. We have hot and cold.

Mike: We'll have the hot ones.

新しい言葉　New Words

- ☐うどん　a type of noodle
- ☐の　one (when identifying something)
- ☐あたたかいの　hot one
- ☐冷たいの　chilled one
- ☐ございますが　We have ____ (the が implies: Which do you prefer?)
- ☐あったかい　warm (casual)

Lesson 4 Lake Biwa is the largest lake in Japan.

[topic]		[place/category]		[adjective]	
琵琶湖	は	日本	で一番	大きい	湖です。
Biwako	wa	Nihon	de ichiban	ōkii	mizuumi desu.

例 Ex. 富士山は日本で一番高い山です。
Fuji-san wa Nihon de ichiban takai yama desu.

日本で一番有名な場所はどこですか？
Nihon de ichiban yūmei na basho wa doko desu ka?

一番好きな音楽はアメリカのロックです。
Ichiban suki na ongaku wa Amerika no rokku desu.

琵琶湖 *Lake Biwa*
湖 *lake*
一番 *number one, the most*
有名な *famous*
場所 *place*
好きな *favorite*

Point!

- 一番 means number one and is used to describe something as *the most* 〈*adjective*〉.
- The adjective itself doesn't change — just put 一番 in front of it.

Dialogue At the post office

ジュン： すみません、これをイギリスに。
局員： イギリスですね。EMSでいいですか？一番早くて保険もあります。ちょっと高いですけど。
ジュン： え～と、一番安い方法は何ですか？
局員： 一番安いのは船便です。でも、３ヵ月かかります。 次に安いのはSAL便で、１、２週間かかります。

Jun: Sumimasen, kore o igirisu ni.
Kyokuin: Igirisu desu ne. EMS de ii desu ka? Ichiban hayakute hoken mo arimasu. Chotto takai desu kedo.
Jun: Ēto, ichiban yasui hōhō wa nan desu ka?
Kyokuin: Ichiban yasui no wa funabin desu. Demo, san-kagetsu kakarimasu. Tsugi ni yasui no wa SAL-bin de, ichi-, ni-shūkan kakarimasu.

Sentences using 一番 can be ordered in different ways depending on context and the focus of the conversation.

(1) クラスで一番かっこいい人は井上君です。
Kurasu de ichiban kakkoii hito wa Inoue-kun desu.
The coolest guy in the class is Inoue.

(2)井上君はクラスの中で一番かっこいい人です。
Inoue-kun wa kurasu no naka de ichiban kakkoii hito desu.
Inoue is the coolest guy in the class.

Chapter 1

They are both correct, but the focus is slightly different—(1) is concerned with who the coolest person in the class is, while (2) is describing 井上君. You can use this expression together with ～の中で to indicate that something is the "best" or "most" out of a group of things.

What's the difference?

一番	一番目	はじめて	はじめに
the most	the first (in a series)	the first time	at first

一番目の料理はサラダです。	はじめて日本に来ました。	はじめに、自己紹介をお願いします。
Ichiban-me no ryōri wa sarada desu.	Hajimete Nihon ni kimashita.	Hajime ni, jikoshōkai o onegai shimasu.
The first dish will be salad.	*This is the first time I've come to Japan.*	*First, please introduce yourself.*

日本で一番のものは？

一番高い山
the highest mountain

Fuji-san

一番きれいな川
the clearest river

Niyodo-gawa

一番人気のかんこうち
the most popular tourist destination

Fushimi-inari

一番高い大仏
the tallest Buddha

Ushiku dai-butsu

Translation

Jun: Excuse me, I would like to send this to England.

Clerk: England? Sure. Would you like to send it using EMS? That is the fastest and it also has insurance. It's a little expensive though.

Jun: Well, what is the cheapest way?

Clerk: The cheapest one is surface mail. But it takes three months. The next cheapest is SAL, which takes one to two weeks.

新しい言葉 New Words

□局員	clerk
□EMS	Express Mail Service
□保険	insurance
□方法	method
□船便	surface mail
□次に	next
□SAL便	Surface Air Lifted

Lesson 5 Osaka is not as famous as Kyoto.

[topic A]		[topic B]		[adjective]	
大阪	は	京都	ほど	有名	じゃないです。
Ōsaka	wa	Kyōto	hodo	yūmei	janai desu.

例 Ex. シンガポールは東京の夏ほど暑くないです。
Shingapōru wa Tōkyō no natsu hodo atsukunai desu.

てんぷらはおすしほど人気じゃない。
Tempura wa o-sushi hodo ninki janai.

僕は君ほど頭がよくない。
Boku wa kimi hodo atama ga yokunai.

てんぷら *a Japanese fried dish*
人気 *popular*
僕 *I (see next page)*
君 *you (see next page)*
頭がよくない *not smart*

Point!

- The adjective comes at the end of the sentence.
- If the topic has already been introduced, the adjective can be omitted.

Shingapōru wa atsui desu ne. *Singapore is hot, isn't it?*
Tōkyō hodo janai desu yo. *Not as much as Tokyo.*

Dialogue Mike and Aoki are talking about their jobs.

マイク：今週も忙しいですか？
青木： ええ、でも先週ほど忙しくないですよ。毎日8時に帰れますから。先週は10時まで仕事でした。
マイク：すごいですね。私も忙しかったけど、青木さんほどじゃないです。日本の会社は大変ですね。

Maiku: Konshū mo isogashii desu ka?
Aoki: Ē, demo senshū hodo isogashikunai desu yo. Mainichi hachi-ji ni kaeremasu kara. Senshū wa ju-ji made shigoto deshita.
Maiku: Sugoi desu ne. Watashi mo isogashikatta kedo, Aoki-san hodo janai desu. Nihon no kaisha wa taihen desu ne.

Making comparisons　くらべてみよう！ Kurabete miyou!

アメリカ人のほうが日本人より背が高いです。 Amerika-jin no hō ga Nihon-jin yori se ga takai desu. *Americans are taller than Japanese people.*	アメリカ人はオランダ人ほど背が高くないです。 Amerika-jin wa Oranda-jin hodo se ga takakunai desu. *Americans are not as tall as Dutch people.*	中国人と日本人は身長が同じくらいです。 Chūgoku-jin to Nihon-jin wa shinchō ga onaji kurai desu. *Chinese people are about the same height as Japanese people.*

The pronouns below are used by men.

ぼく	きみ	おれ	おまえ
boku	kimi	ore	omae
I	*You*	*I*	*You*

ぼくsounds soft, humble, and educated. It is typically used by children, students (in a class), doctors, and professors. おれ carries a sense of masculinity. It is used by men in general (outside of classes, offices, and similar settings). きみ and おまえ both mean *you* and are used in the same way as ぼく and おれ respectively.

Other expressions using ほど

それほどでもないです。 Sore hodo demo nai desu. *Not really.*	行くほどじゃないです。 Iku hodo janai desu. *It's not worth it to go.*	思ったほどじゃないです。 Omotta hodo janai desu. *Not as much I thought.*

Translation

Mike: Are you busy this week too?

Aoki: Yes, but not as busy as last week. I can leave at eight every day. I had to work until ten last week.

Mike: Wow. I was busy too, but not as much as you. Japanese companies are rough.

新しい言葉 New Words

- □会社　company, office
- □大変　rough, hard

Lesson 6 I feel better now.

[adjective]

今は　気分が　よく　なりました。

Ima wa kibun ga　yoku　narimashita.

例 Ex. 部屋がきれいになりました。
Heya ga kirei ni narimashita.

すっかり寒くなりましたね。
Sukkari samuku narimashita ne.

7月になりました。
Shichi-gatsu ni narimashita.

今は *now* (は *is used for comparison, comparing now to before*)
気分 *feeling*
なりました (なる) *became*
よくなりました (いい＋なる) *got better*
すっかり *completely*

Point!

● i-adjectives:	かわいい	→	かわいく なる
● na-adjectives:	きれい	→	きれい に なる
● Nouns:	7月	→	7月 に なる

Dialogue Mike is talking with his neighbor about her daughter.

マイク：娘さん、大きくなりましたね。
小川：　ええ、来年、高校生になりますよ。
マイク：もう高校生ですか。はやいですね。
小川：　ほんとに。マイクさんの日本語も上手になりましたね。
マイク：ありがとうございます。

Maiku: Musume-san, ōkiku narimashita ne.
Ogawa: Ē, rainen kōkōsei ni narimasu yo.
Maiku: Mō kōkōsei desu ka. Hayai desu ne.
Ogawa: Honto ni. Maiku-san no nihongo mo jōzu ni narimashita ne.
Maiku: Arigatō gozaimasu.

Common Expressions

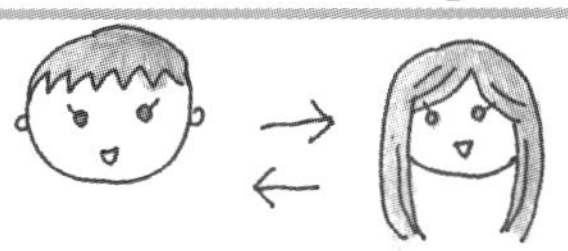

髪が短くなる
kami ga mijikaku naru

髪が長くなる
kami ga nagaku naru

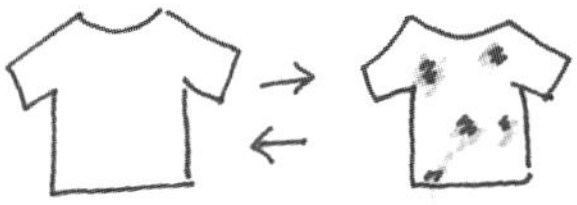

きれいになる
kirei ni naru

汚くなる
kitanaku naru

ひまになる
hima ni naru

いそがしくなる
isogashiku naru

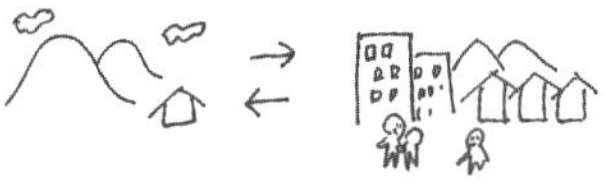

しずかになる
shizuka ni naru

にぎやかになる
nigiyaka ni naru

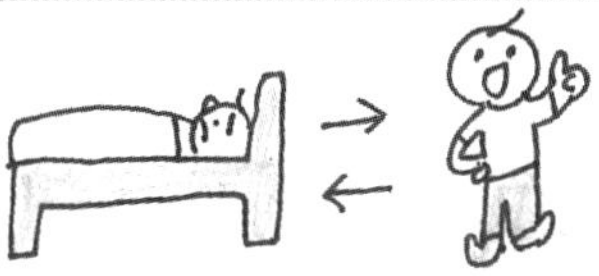

病気になる
byōki ni naru

元気になる
genki ni naru

意地悪になる
ijiwaru ni naru

親切になる
shinsetsu ni naru

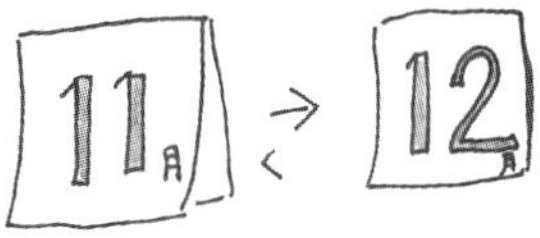

１２月になる
jūni-gatsu ni naru

春になる
haru ni naru

二十歳になる・大人になる
hatachi ni naru / otona ni naru

Watch out!

× 古くなる
furuku naru
(can't use with people)

もう年です。
Mō toshi desu.

× ふとくなる
futoku naru
use the verb ふとる instead

太りました。
Futorimashita.

Other expressions with たいです

有名になりたいです。
Yūmei ni naritai desu.
I want to become famous.

お金持ちになりたいです。
O-kanemochi ni naritai desu.
I want to become a rich person.

ミュージシャンになりたかったです。
Myūjishan ni naritakatta desu.
I wanted to become a musician.

Translation

Mike: Your daughter has gotten big.

Ogawa: Yes, she will be a high-school student next year.

Mike: Is she already a high-school student? They grow up so fast.

Ogawa: It's true. Your Japanese has gotten better, too.

Mike: Thank you so much.

新しい言葉 New Words

- □娘さん　your daughter
- □高校生　high-school student
- □はやい　(grow up) fast

Lesson 7 It looks delicious!

[adjective]

おいし	そうですね。
Oishi	sō desu ne.

例 Ex. たのしそうですね。
Tanoshi sō desu ne.

あの人は親切そうです。
Ano hito wa shinsetsu sō desu.

このパソコンはよくなさそうです。
Kono pasokon wa yokunasa sō desu.

そう *looks / sounds*
よくなさそう *doesn't look good*
よくない *not good*

Point!

- i-adjectives: たのしい → たのしそう
- na-adjectives: 親切 → 親切そう
- Negative: たのしくない → たのしくなさそう
  親切じゃない → 親切じゃなさそう
- そう is not used after nouns—use っぽい instead.
  (日本人っぽい *looks like a Japanese person.*)
- There is no pause when pronouncing these conjugations —say them as if they are single words.

Dialogue

マイク：これ、先週の旅行の写真です。
青木：わあ、ごうかそうなホテルですね。
この料理はおいしそうですね。なんですか？
マイク：名前は覚えてませんけど、おいしかったです。
青木：これはマイクさんの彼女ですか？優しそうですね。

Maiku: Kore, senshū no ryokō no shashin desu.
Aoki: Waa, gōkasōna hoteru desu ne. Kono ryōri wa oishisō desu ne. Nan desu ka?
Maiku: Namae wa oboetemasen kedo, oishikatta desu.
Aoki: Kore wa Maiku-san no kanojo desu ka? Yasashi sō desu ne.

What's the difference? おいしそう vs. おいしいそう

そうです can also be used in a different way (see the chapter on Plain Style for more information):

おいしそうです。
Oishi sō desu.
That looks delicious.

おいしいそうです。
Oishii sō desu.
I heard that this is delicious.

Notice that with the expression on the right, the i-adjective is not conjugated—the そうです follows the standard form. With na-adjectives, put だ before そうです.

Here are a few more examples of this other そうです usage:

明日は寒いそうです。
Ashita wa samui sō desu.
I heard tomorrow will be cold.

東京はにぎやかだそうです。
Tōkyō wa nigiyaka dasō desu.
They say that Tokyo is lively.

Exceptions!

- かわいい doesn't conjugate, because かわいそう has a completely different meaning: *pitiful*.

- いい becomes よさそう.

But don't use that to respond to a question. You can simply say いいですね to accept an invitation.

Sounds good!

そうです is also used with verbs:

雨が降りそうです。
Ame ga furi sō desu.
Looks like rain.

雨が降るそうです。
Ame ga furu sō desu.
I heard it will rain.

Translation

Mike: These are the pictures from my trip last week.

Aoki: Wow, this hotel looks splendid. And this food looks delicious. What is it?

Mike: I don't remember the name, but it was delicious.

Aoki: Is this your girlfriend? She looks nice.

新しい言葉 New Words

□ごうか splendid

Lesson 8

More Adjectives

1. Here are some other commonly used na-adjectives:

好き	嫌い	上手	下手	得意	苦手
suki	kirai	jōzu	heta	tokui	nigate
like	*hate*	*good at*	*bad at*	*good at (modest)*	*bad at (modest)*

例 Ex. 好きな歌は「Let it Be」です。
Suki na uta wa "Let it Be" desu. *My favorite song is "Let it Be."*

得意なことは空手です。
Tokui na koto wa, karate desu. *I'm pretty good at karate.*

Point!

- English uses transitive verbs to express likes, dislikes and wants, but these concepts are adjectives in Japanese.

2. To express a desire, use ほしい for nouns and たい for verbs.

例 Ex. お金がほしいです。
O-kane ga hoshii desu. *I want some money.*

日本語を勉強したいです。
Nihongo o benkyō shitai desu. *I want to study Japanese.*

ほしい and たい are conjugated in the same way as other i-adjectives.

ほしくないです。	*I don't want it.*
ほしかったです。	*I wanted it.*
ほしくなかったです。	*I didn't want it.*

行きたくないです。	*I don't want to go.*
行きたかったです。	*I wanted to go.*
行きたくなかったです。	*I didn't want to go.*

To make adjectives casual, follow the guide below:

大きいです	→	大きい
大きくないです	→	大きくない
親切です	→	親切だ
親切じゃないです	→	親切じゃない
親切でした	→	親切だった
親切じゃなかったです	→	親切じゃなかった

* よ is used when you provide information that you think the listener doesn't know.
ね indicates your agreement or shows that you are impressed.

Chapter 2

Verbs

第 2 章　動詞文

Verbs

In the first book of this series, we learned the masu-form, te-form, ta-form, and potential form of verbs. We will now look at some additional ways they can be used and learn some other forms that verbs can take.

ますけい	(masu-form)	polite present and future tense	*do; will do*
じしょけい	(dictionary form)	informal present and future tense	*do; will do*
ないけい	(nai-form)	informal negative present and future tense	*don't; won't*
たけい	(ta-form)	informal past tense	*didn't; haven't*
てけい	(te-form)	requests, asking permission, progressive tense	*am doing; may I*
かのうけい	(potential form)	ability	*can do*
いこうけい	(volitional form)	suggestions	*let's do*

How do we conjugate these forms?

Every verb belongs to one of three groups:
Group 1: dictionary form of the verb ends with [u] (*u* verbs)
Group 2: dictionary form ends with [eru] or [iru] (*ru* verbs)
Group 3: verbs with irregular conjugations (only two exist— 来る and する)

So if the dictionary form of the verb ends in る , it belongs to Group 2?

Not always. Some Group 1 verbs like とる , のる , and かえる also end in る .

Well, how can I know which group a verb belongs to?

To do this, you can either memorize the verb's masu-form or its nai-form.

たべる → たべます Group 2 because the final る is dropped.
とる → とります Group 1 because the final る becomes り .
たべる → たべない Group 2 because the final る is dropped.
とる → とらない Group 1 because the final る is becomes ら .

Group 1

nai-form: a	masu-form: i	dictionary form: u	potential form: e	volitional form: o
行かない	行きます	行く	行ける	行こう
ikanai	ikimasu	iku	ikeru	ikou

To conjugate Group 2 verbs, add one of the endings in the table below to the verb stem.

Group 2

nai-form	masu-form	dictionary form	potential form	volitional form
食べない	食べます	食べる	食べられる	食べよう
tabenai	tabemasu	taberu	taberareru	tabeyou

Just memorize the conjugations for the two irregular verbs in Group 3.

Group 3

nai-form	masu-form	dictionary form	potential form	volitional form
しない	します	する	できる	しよう
shinai	shimasu	suru	dekiru	shiyou
こない	きます	くる	こられる	こよう
konai	kimasu	kuru	korareru	koyou

The conjugations for te-form and ta-form follow a different set of rules. We will examine those in detail later in this chapter.

ますけい masu-form

ますけい is used in formal conversation and writing. This is the form that strangers most often use when communicating with each other.

For Group 1 verbs, the sound that comes before ます is always [i] (whether the single character い or a syllable that ends in it like り or み). For Group 2 verbs, the sound before ます is always either [i] or [e].

Verbs with similar endings in dictionary form follow the same pattern when changing to masu-form.

Some Group 1 verbs masquerade as Group 2 verbs because they also end with る , but when they are conjugated to masu-form that る becomes り . For example, the Group 1 verb 眠る (to sleep or fall asleep) changes to 眠ります , while the Group 2 verb 寝る (to lie down or go to bed) becomes 寝ます .

Group 1

	dictionary form		masu-form	
to meet	会う	au	会います	aimasu
to sing	歌う	utau	歌います	utaimasu
to buy	買う	kau	買います	kaimasu
to say	言う	iu	言います	iimasu
to differ	違う	chigau	違います	chigaimasu
to pay	払う	harau	払います	haraimasu
to use	使う	tsukau	使います	tsukaimasu
to hold	持つ	motsu	持ちます	mochimasu
to wait	待つ	matsu	待ちます	machimasu
to stand	立つ	tatsu	立ちます	tachimasu
to take	取る	toru	取ります	torimasu
to enter	入る	hairu	入ります	hairimasu
to make	作る	tsukuru	作ります	tsukurimasu
to send	送る	okuru	送ります	okurimasu
to know	知る	shiru	知ります	shirimasu
to ride	乗る	noru	乗ります	norimasu
to cut	切る	kiru	切ります	kirimasu
to be troubled	困る	komaru	困ります	komarimasu
to return	帰る	kaeru	帰ります	kaerimasu
to climb	登る	noboru	登ります	noborimasu
to sleep	眠る	nemuru	眠ります	nemurimasu
to choose	選ぶ	erabu	選びます	erabimasu
to carry	運ぶ	hakobu	運びます	hakobimasu
to call	呼ぶ	yobu	呼びます	yobimasu

to fall	転ぶ	korobu	転びます	korobimasu
to live	住む	sumu	住みます	sumimasu
to be crowded	混む	komu	混みます	komimasu
to read	読む	yomu	読みます	yomimasu
to rest	休む	yasumu	休みます	yasumimasu
to write	書く	kaku	書きます	kakimasu
to arrive	着く	tsuku	着きます	tsukimasu
to hear/listen/ask	聞く	kiku	聞きます	kikimasu
to walk	歩く	aruku	歩きます	arukimasu
to swim	泳ぐ	oyogu	泳ぎます	oyogimasu
to hurry	急ぐ	isogu	急ぎます	isogimasu
to hand or pass	渡す	watasu	渡します	watashimasu
to lend or rent	貸す	kasu	貸します	kashimasu
to give back	返す	kaesu	返します	kaeshimasu
to look for	探す	sagasu	探します	sagashimasu
to talk or speak	話す	hanasu	話します	hanashimasu

Group 2

	dictionary form		masu-form	
to wake	起きる	okiru	起きます	okimasu
to go to bed	寝る	neru	寝ます	nemasu
to open	開ける	akeru	開けます	akemasu
to close	閉める	shimeru	閉めます	shimemasu
to put in	入れる	ireru	入れます	iremasu
to see/look/watch	見る	miru	見ます	mimasu
to teach	教える	oshieru	教えます	oshiemasu
to show	見せる	miseru	見せます	misemasu
to stop	止める	tomeru	止めます	tomemasu
to forget	忘れる	wasureru	忘れます	wasuremasu
to wear	着る	kiru	着ます	kimasu

Group 3

	dictionary form		masu-form	
to do	する	suru	します	shimasu
to come	来る	kuru	来ます	kimasu

Lesson 9 I'm going to the convenience store to buy a bento.

	[masu-stem]	[verb]
コンビニにお弁当を	買い	に行きます。
Konbini ni o-bentō o	kai	ni ikimasu.

例 Ex. 渋谷に映画を見に行きます。
Shibuya ni eiga o mi ni ikimasu.

京都に日本文化を勉強しに来ました。
Kyōto ni nihon bunka o benkyō shi ni kimashita.

駅に友達を迎えに行きます。
Eki ni tomodachi o mukae ni ikimasu.

コンビニ	*convenience store*
お弁当（べんとう）	*boxed lunch*
渋谷	*a famous place in Tokyo*
文化	*culture*
迎え（むかえる）	*to pick up*

Point!

- Use this structure when you want to express your purpose for going or coming.
- You need to say the particle に twice: place に purpose に ikimasu.
- Sometimes there can be even more than two に, for example:
  日本に友達に会いに行きます。 *I'll go to Japan to meet my friend.*
  Nihon ni tomodachi ni ai ni ikimasu.

Dialogue Nick has just left his teacher's house when he receives a phone call.

先生：	もしもし、ニックさん。家に本を忘れましたよ。	**Sensei:**	Moshimoshi, Nikku-san. Uchi ni hon o wasuremashita yo.
ニック：	あ、すみません。すぐ取りに行きます。	**Nikku:**	A, sumimasen. Sugu tori ni ikimasu.
ニック：	先生、本を取りに来ました。	**Nikku:**	Sensei, hon o tori ni kimashita.
先生：	はい、どうぞ。また遊びに来てくださいね。	**Sensei:**	Hai dōzo. Mata asobi ni kite kudasai ne.
ニック：	ありがとうございます！ 失礼します。	**Nikku:**	Arigatō gozaimasu. Shitsurei shimasu.

Common Expressions

What's the difference? うち vs. いえ

Family:	うちの子供 uchi no kodomo	うちのお母さん uchi no okāsan	うちのお父さん uchi no otōsan
Organizations:	うちの会社 uchi no kaisha	うちの学校 uchi no gakkō	うちのグループ uchi no gurūpu
People around you:	うちの部長 uchi no buchō	うちの先生 uchi no sensei	うちのメンバー uchi no menbā

English speakers use *my* for these expressions, which equates to 私の in Japanese; but this sounds too personal or familiar for Japanese people.

Translation

Teacher: Hello, Nick, you forgot your book at my place.

Nick: Oh, Thank you. I'll come to get it right now.

Nick: Professor, I came here to get my book.

Teacher: Here you go. Come and hang out again sometime.

Nick: Thank you so much! Sorry to bother you.

新しい言葉 New Words

- ☐忘れましたよ（わすれる） you forgot
- ☐取り（とる） to get
- ☐遊び（あそぶ） to hang out

Lesson 10 Let's talk over a cup of coffee.

	[masu-stem]		[verb]
コーヒーを	飲み	ながら、	話しませんか？
Kōhī o	nomi	nagara,	hanashimasen ka?

例 Ex. テレビをみながらご飯をたべます。
Terebi o minagara gohan o tabemasu.

音楽を聞きながら勉強できません。
Ongaku o kikinagara benkyō dekimasen.

４月から働きながら大学に行きます。
Shi-gatsu kara hatarakinagara daigaku ni ikimasu.

ながら	*while; during*
いつも	*always*

Point!

- Use ながら to describe doing two activities at the same time.
- The masu-stem of a verb must come before ながら, but any verb conjugation is possible in the part that follows.
- ながら constructions always contain two verbs, with the second verb being the more important one. For example, if you listen to music while driving, you would say 音楽を聞きながら運転します (ongaku o kikinagara unten shimasu) since driving is the main action.

Dialogue Jenna and her teacher are heading to the station after class.

ジェナ：先生、ちょっと相談したいことがあります。
先生：ええ。そこでお茶でも飲みながら話しましょう。
—ジェナがサインに気づく—
ジェナ：先生、歩きスマホってなんですか？
先生：歩きながらスマートフォンを使うっていう意味ですよ。
ジェナ：なるほど。

Jena: Sensei, chotto sōdan shitai koto ga arimasu.
Sensei: Ē, soko de ocha demo nominagara hanashimashō.
— Jena ga sain ni kizuku —
Jena: Sensei, aruki sumaho tte nan desu ka?
Sensei: Arukinagara sumāto-fon o tsukau tte iu imi desu yo.
Jenna: Naruhodo.

What's the difference? あいだ vs. ながら

仕事の間に、お菓子を食べます。
Shigoto no aida ni, okashi o tabemasu.
I eat sweets at work sometimes.

仕事をしながら、お菓子をたべます。
Shigoto o shinagara, okashi o tabemasu.
I eat sweets the entire time I'm working.

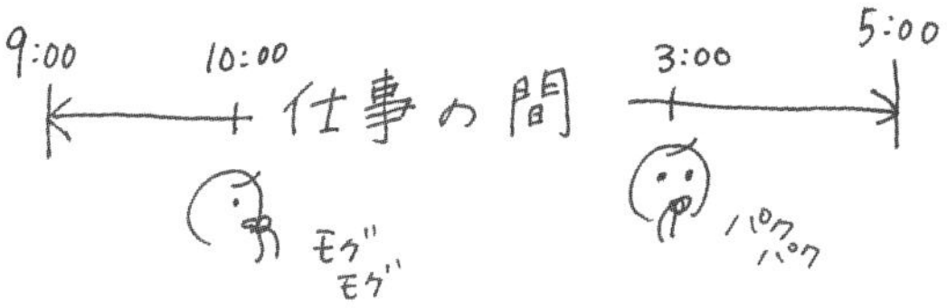

You can't use ながら if two verbs have **different subjects**. For that, you can use 間.

雨が降っている間、うちにいました。
Ame ga futte iru aida, uchi ni imashita.
I was at home while it was raining.

Other Expressions

ケーキでも食べませんか　Kēki demo tabemasen ka?
Would you like to eat some cake or something?

This でも means *or something* and is used after nouns.

Don't confuse the above でも with the one that means *but* at the beginning of a sentence.

お茶が好きです。でも、コーヒーは好きじゃないです。
Ocha ga suki desu. Demo, kōhī wa suki janai desu. *I like tea. But I don't like coffee.*

～とは　なんですか

とは is used when asking about or explaining the meaning of words. It is often shortened to って.

Translation

Jenna: I have something that I want to discuss with you.

Teacher: Sure, shall we talk over a cup of tea or something?

— Jenna notices a sign —

Jenna: What is *aruki sumaho*?

Teacher: It means using your phone while you are walking.

Jenna: Oh, I see.

新しい言葉 New Words

- □相談　discuss, consultation
- □スマホ　smartphone
- □ってなんですか　What does ___ mean?
- □っていう意味です　It means ___
- □なるほど　I see; makes sense

Lesson 11 Please show me how to use this machine.

[masu-stem] [verb]

この機械の **使い** 方を教えてください。

Kono kikai no **tsukai** kata o oshiete kudasai.

例 Ex. 申し込み方が分かりません。
Mōshikomikata ga wakarimasen.

この料理の食べ方を教えてください。
Kono ryōri no tabekata o oshiete kudasai.

カレーライスの作り方を知りたいです。
Karē-raisu no tsukurikata o shiritai desu.

機械 *machine*
方（かた） *way; method*
教えて（おしえる） *to teach; to show*
申し込み（もうしこむ） *to apply; to register; to sign up*
カレーライス *curry and rice*

Point!

- The 方 that follows the masu-stem can also be written in hiragana (かた).
- 知る (to know), 分かる (to understand), and 教える (to tell or teach) are some verbs that commonly used with ~かた.

Dialogue Jimmy is asking his friend how to read a kanji character.

ジミー： この漢字の読み方を教えてください。
大野： はい、いいですよ。
ジミー： 漢字のいい覚え方がありますか？
大野： うーん、そうですね。私は毎日たくさん漢字を書きましたね。
ジミー： 書き方はあきらめました。読み方を覚えたいです。
大野： そうだ、外国人用の漢字のアプリがたくさんありますよ。

Jimī: Kono kanji no yomikata o oshiete kudasai.
Ōno: Hai, ii desu yo.
Jimī: Kanji no ii oboekata ga arimasu ka?
Ōno: Ūn, sō desu ne. Watashi wa mainichi takusan kanji o kakimashita ne.
Jimī: Kakikata wa akirame-mashita. Yomikata o oboetai desu.
Ōno: Sō da, gaikokujin-yō no kanji no apuri ga takusan arimasu yo.

Various Expressions

おはしの使い方はむずかしいです。
O-hashi no tsukaikata wa muzukashii desu.
Using chopsticks is difficult.

やり方を間違えました。
Yarikata o machigaemashita.
I did it the wrong way.

口の利き方が悪いですよ。
Kuchi no kikikata ga warui desu yo.
You shouldn't talk that way.

一番かんたんな行き方を教えてください。
Ichiban kantan na ikikata o oshiete kudasai.
Can you tell me the easiest way to get there?

行き方 Directions

まっすぐ
massugu
straight

曲がる
magaru
to turn

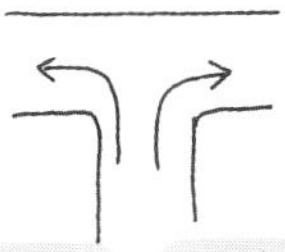

止まる
tomaru
to stop

ここで止まってください。
Koko de tomatte kudasai.
Please stop here.

まっすぐ行ってください。
Massugu itte kudasai.
Please go straight.

左
hidari
left

右
migi
right

右に曲がってください。
Migi ni magatte kudasai.
Please turn right.

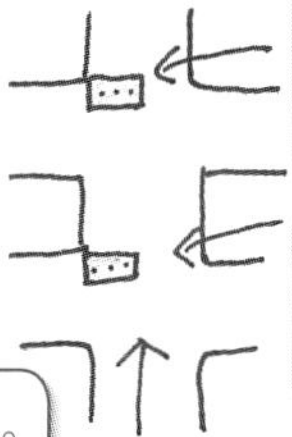

二つ目
futatsu-me
the second

一つ目
hitotsu-me
the first

信号
shingō
traffic light

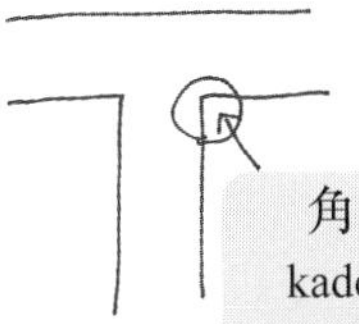

角
kado
corner

二つ目の信号で左に曲がってください。
Futatsu-me no shingō de hidari ni magatte kudasai.
Please turn left at the second light.

Translation

Jimmy: Can you teach me how to read this kanji?
Ōno: Sure.
Jimmy: Is there a good way to memorize kanji characters?
Ōno: Well, I wrote a bunch of kanji every day.
Jimmy: I gave up on writing...I want to memorize the pronunciations.
Ōno: Oh, there are many kanji apps for foreigners.

新しい言葉 New Words

□あきらめました（あきらめる） gave up
□たいです（たい） want to ____
□用 used for; intended for
□アプリ (software) application

Lesson 12 It is hard to understand.

[masu-stem]	[verb]
わかり	にくいです。
Wakari	nikui desu.

例 Ex. この本は読みやすいです。
Kono hon wa yomiyasui desu.

このパソコンは使いにくいです。
Kono pasokon wa tsukainikui desu.

この薬は苦いから飲みづらいです。
Kono kusuri wa nigai kara nomizurai desu.

にくい・づらい *difficult/hard to ______*
やすい *easy to ______*
薬 *medicine*
苦い *bitter*

Point!

- There is no real difference between にくい and づらい. However, にくい can be used with any verb, while some verbs are never used with づらい. When in doubt, stick with にくい.
- As a standalone adjective, やすい means inexpensive. There are adjectives in Japanese that mean easy (かんたん, やさしい, etc.) but they are not used in this grammar construction.

Dialogue Sena is working for a Japanese company. Ōno is her co-worker.

セナ： あの、ちょっとこのパソコン使ってもいいですか？
大野： いいですよ。日本語だから使いづらいでしょうけど…
セナ： 漢字が読みにくいので大きくしてもいいですか？
大野： もちろん。
セナ： ああ、読みやすくなりました。

Sena: Ano, chotto kono pasokon tsukatte mo ii desu ka?
Ōno: Ii desu yo. Nihongo dakara tsukaizurai deshō kedo…
Sena: Kanji ga yominikui node ōkiku shite mo ii desu ka?
Ōno: Mochiron.
Sena: Aa, yomiyasuku narimashita.

Common expressions

持ちやすい
mochiyasui

飲みやすい
nomiyasui

書きやすい
kakiyasui

履きやすい
hakiyasui

説明しにくい
setsumei shinikui

食べにくい
tabenikui

開けにくい
akenikui

見つけにくい
mitsukenikui

Other expressions

Sometimes when やすい follows a verb, it means that the action happens often and carries a negative nuance. And in rare cases, にくい can imply a positive aspect, in which case づらい is never used.

怒りやすい
okoriyasui

忘れやすい
wasureyasui

割れにくい
warenikui

壊れにくい
kowarenikui

Watch out!

You can't say 勉強しにくい to express that something is difficult to learn—in that case, say 分かりにくい or simply 難しい. If you would like to say that the act of studying is difficult, you need to give a specific reason.

家はうるさくて、勉強しにくいです。
Uchi wa urusakute benkyō shinikui desu.
My house is noisy so it is hard to study there.

漢字は覚えにくい。
Kanji wa oboenikui.
Kanji are hard to memorize.

Translation

Sena: Excuse me, may I use this computer for a minute?

Ōno: Sure, but it might be difficult to use because it's in Japanese.

Sena: Is it OK if I make the font bigger since the kanji is hard to read?

Ōno: Of course.

Sena: Ahh, now it is easier to read.

新しい言葉 New Words

□大きくする　make bigger

Lesson 13 I started attending a language school in April.

	[masu-stem]	[verb]
4月から語学学校に	通い	始めました。
Shi-gatsu kara gogaku gakkō ni	kayoi	hajimemashita.

例 Ex. 話し始めました。
Hanashi hajimemashita.

話し続けました。
Hanashi tsuzukemashita.

話し終わりました。
Hanashi owarimashita.

通い（かよう）	*to attend work, school*
始めました（はじめる）	*started*
続けました（つづける）	*continued*
終わりました（おわる）	*finished*

Point!

- You can change the tense of the verb on the end to match the situation:

もうすぐ食べ終わります。
Mō sugu tabe owarimasu. *We'll be done eating soon.*

7時半に宿題をやり始めます。
Shichi-ji han ni shukudai o yari hajimemasu.
I'll start doing my homework at 7:30.

Dialogue Aoki is meeting Lucas to return a book he borrowed.

青木：	ルーカスさん、久しぶりですね。この本、読み終わりました。ありがとうございます。	**Aoki:**	Rūcasu-san, hisashiburi desu ne. Kono hon, yomi owarimashita. Arigatō gozaimasu.
ルーカス：	大学の論文は書き終わりましたか？	**Rūkasu:**	Daigaku no ronbun wa kaki owarimashita ka?
青木：	ええ、おかげさまで。ルーカスさんは最近どうですか？	**Aoki:**	Ē, o-kagesama de. Rūkasu-san wa saikin dō desu ka?
ルーカス：	4月から近くの工場で働き始めました。大変ですけど、家族のために働き続けますよ。	**Rūkasu:**	Shi-gatsu kara chikaku no kōjō de hataraki hajimemashita.Taihen desu kedo, kazoku no tame ni hataraki tsuzukemasu yo.

What's the difference? はじめる vs. だす

There's a similar expression to the one we just learned, but it uses だす.

先生が話し始めました。
Sensei ga hanashi hajime-mashita.
My teacher started speaking.

先生が話しだしました。
Sensei ga hanashi dashi-mashita.
My teacher started speaking.

The difference is that だす is used when the action happens abruptly or unexpectedly. This is why ～だす is often paired with the adverb きゅうに (suddenly) and ～始める with やっと (finally).

彼女は急に話しだしました。
Kanojo wa kyū ni hanashi dashimashita.
She suddenly started talking.

彼女はやっと話し始めました。
Kanojo wa yatto hanashi hajiemashita.
She finally started talking.

Here are some other examples that use だす:

赤ちゃんが急に泣きだしました。
Akachan ga kyū ni naki dashi-mashita.
The baby suddenly started crying.

妻が急に怒りだしました。
Tsuma ga kyū ni okori dashi-mashita.
My wife got angry all of a sudden.

子供が急に飛びだしました。
Kodomo ga kyū ni tobi dashi-mashita.
Out of nowhere, the child darted out.

Watch out!

You can't use ～終わる with certain verbs. A common mistake is to use it to indicate that the rain has stopped, but there is a special verb for that:

雨がやみました。
Ame ga yamimashita.
The rain has stopped.

Translation

Aoki: Lucas, it's been a while.
I finished reading this book. Thank you.

Lucas: Did you finish writing your college report?

Aoki: Yes, thanks to you. How have you been lately, Lucas?

Lucas: I started working at a nearby factory in April.
It's hard, but I'll keep working for my family's sake.

新しい言葉 New Words

- □久しぶり it's been a while
- □論文 report
- □おかげさまで thanks to you
- □最近 recently
- □工場 factory
- □大変 hard
- □のために for
- □働き（はたらく） to work

Lesson 14 I ate too much yesterday!

[masu-stem] [verb]

昨日 **食べ** すぎました。

Kinō **tabe** sugimashita.

例 Ex. ゲームをしすぎて学校に遅れました。
Gēmu o shisugite gakkō ni okuremashita.

昨日は寝すぎました。
Kinō wa nesugimashita.

考えすぎですよ。
Kangaesugi desu yo.

すぎる *to excess; too much*
寝すぎて(ねる) *sleep too much*
考えすぎ (かんがえる) *overthink*
ゲーム *video game*

Point!

- This expression is mostly used for negative things.
- すぎる is a verb, but its masu-stem is sometimes used as a noun:
  考えすぎます = 考えすぎです

Dialogue Ōki is getting a checkup at the clinic.

医者： ちょっと血糖値が高いですね。
飲みすぎ、食べ過ぎに気をつけて。

大木： 最近食欲がないし、お酒もそんなに……

医者： 働きすぎじゃないですか？

大木： ええ、毎日残業がありますね。土日も時々仕事があります。

医者： それはよくないですね。

Isha: Chotto kettōchi ga takai desu ne. Nomisugi, tabesugi ni ki o tsukete.

Ōki: Saikin shokuyoku ga nai shi, o-sake mo sonna ni...

Isha: Hatarakisugi janai desu ka?

Ōki: Ē, mainichi zangyō ga arimasu ne. Donichi mo tokidoki shigoto ga arimasu.

Isha: Sore wa yokunai desu ne.

すぎる can also be used with adjectives.

高すぎる
takasugiru

安すぎる
yasusugiru

大きすぎる
ōkisugiru

小さすぎる
chīsasugiru

ひますぎる
himasugiru

いそがしすぎる
isogashisugiru

強すぎる
tsuyosugiru

弱すぎる
yowasugiru

難しすぎる
muzukashisugiru

簡単すぎる
kantansugiru

辛すぎる
karasugiru

甘すぎる
amasugiru

Common Expressions

辛すぎて食べられない。
Karasugite taberarenai.
It's too spicy, so I can't eat it.

高すぎて買えない。
Takasugite kaenai.
It's too expensive, so I can't buy it.

Watch out!

You can't use すぎる for actions that will happen in the future.

× 明日は飲みすぎます。
Ashita wa nomisugimasu.
I will drink too much tomorrow.

◯ いつも飲みすぎます。
Itsumo nomisugimasu.
I always drink too much.

すぎる also can't be used to express positive things.

× 来週テストがあるから、勉強しすぎます。
Raishū tesuto ga aru kara, benkyō shisugimasu.
There is a test next week, so I will study too much.

◯ 来週テストがあるから、たくさん勉強します。
Raishū tesuto ga aru kara, takusan benkyō shimasu.
There is a test next week, so I will study a lot.

Translation

Doctor: Your blood-sugar level is a little high. Be careful about drinking and eating too much.

Ooki: I have no appetite lately, and I'm not drinking alcohol that much...

Doctor: Are you working too much?

Ooki: Yes, I work overtime everyday. Sometimes even on weekends, too.

Doctor: That's not good.

新しい言葉 New Words

- □血糖値 blood-sugar level
- □気をつけて be careful
- □食欲 appetite
- □そんなに not really
- □働きすぎ work too much
- □残業 overtime

じしょけい / ないけい Dictionary form / nai-form

As its name suggests, dictionary form is the form in which verbs are listed in the dictionary. It is the primary verb tense used to end present- and future-tense sentences in informal conversation, although it also appears in literature and other writing. The dictionary form corresponds to the infinite verb form in English and is employed in many of the same ways within sentences. The lessons in this chapter will introduce some of these usages.

nai-form is simply the negative version of dictionary form and is created according to the patterns in the below table.

Group 1

	dictionary form		nai-form	
to meet	会う	au	会わない	awanai
to sing	歌う	utau	歌わない	utawanai
to buy	買う	kau	買わない	kawanai
to say	言う	iu	言わない	iwanai
to differ	違う	chigau	違わない	chigawanai
to pay	払う	harau	払わない	harawanai
to use	使う	tsukau	使わない	tsukawanai
to hold	持つ	motsu	持たない	motanai
to wait	待つ	matsu	待たない	matanai
to stand	立つ	tatsu	立たない	tatanai
to take	取る	toru	取らない	toranai
to enter	入る	hairu	入らない	hairanai
to make	作る	tsukuru	作らない	tsukuranai
to send	送る	okuru	送らない	okuranai
to know	知る	shiru	知らない	shiranai
to ride	乗る	noru	乗らない	noranai
to cut	切る	kiru	切らない	kiranai
to be troubled	困る	komaru	困らない	komaranai
to return	帰る	kaeru	帰らない	kaeranai
to climb	登る	noboru	登らない	noboranai
to sleep	眠る	nemuru	眠らない	nemuranai
to choose	選ぶ	erabu	選ばない	erabanai
to carry	運ぶ	hakobu	運ばない	hakobanai
to call	呼ぶ	yobu	呼ばない	yobanai
to fall	転ぶ	korobu	転ばない	korobanai
to live	住む	sumu	住まない	sumanai
to be crowded	混む	komu	混まない	komanai

to read	読む	yomu	読まない	yomanai
to rest	休む	yasumu	休まない	yasumanai
to write	書く	kaku	書かない	kakanai
to arrive	着く	tsuku	着かない	tsukanai
to hear/listen/ask	聞く	kiku	聞かない	kikanai
to walk	歩く	aruku	歩かない	arukanai
to swim	泳ぐ	oyogu	泳がない	oyoganai
to hurry	急ぐ	isogu	急がない	isoganai
to hand or pass	渡す	watasu	渡さない	watasanai
to lend or rent	貸す	kasu	貸さない	kasanai
to give back	返す	kaesu	返さない	kaesanai
to look for	探す	sagasu	探さない	sagasanai
to talk or speak	話す	hanasu	話さない	hanasanai

Group 2

	dictionary form		nai-form	
to wake	起きる	okiru	起きない	okinai
to sleep	寝る	neru	寝ない	nenai
to open	開ける	akeru	開けない	akenai
to close	閉める	shimeru	閉めない	shimenai
to put in	入れる	ireru	入れない	irenai
to see/look/watch	見る	miru	見ない	minai
to teach	教える	oshieru	教えない	oshienai
to show	見せる	miseru	見せない	misenai
to stop	止める	tomeru	止めない	tomenai
to forget	忘れる	wasureru	忘れない	wasurenai
to wear	着る	kiru	着ない	kinai

Group 3

	dictionary form		nai-form	
to do	する	suru	しない	shinai
to come	来る	kuru	来ない	konai

Lesson 15 Want some coffee?

[dictionary or nai-form]

コーヒー	飲む	?
Kōhī	nomu	?

例 Ex. 夏休み、海に行かない？
Natsuyasumi, umi ni ikanai?

友達と一緒に行くよ。
Tomodachi to issho ni iku yo.

お母さんに誕生日プレゼントあげる。
Okāsan ni tanjōbi purezento ageru.

友達と	*with my friend(s)*
夏休み	*summer vacation*
海	*beach; sea; ocean*
一緒に	*together with*
誕生日	*birthday*
プレゼント	*present*
あげる	*to give*

Point!

- In casual conversation, the question marker か is often omitted; to indicate a question, raise the tone of the final syllable instead.
- Particles are typically omitted unless doing so would cause confusion.

Dialogue Kana and Miki are discussing which movie to see.

かな：ねー、これ見る？	**Kana:** Nē, kore miru?
みき：えー、それ恐いよ。	**Miki:** Ē, sore kowai yo.
かな：そっか…こっちにする？	**Kana:** Sokka...kocchi ni suru?
みき：いや、これはつまんないよ。	**Miki:** Iya, kore wa tsumannai yo.
かな：じゃ、どれ見るの？	**Kana:** Ja, dore miru no?
みき：えーと……	**Miki:** Ēto...

Watch out!

Questions: raise the pitch of the final syllable   Answers: drop the pitch of the final syllable slightly

Some casual expressions

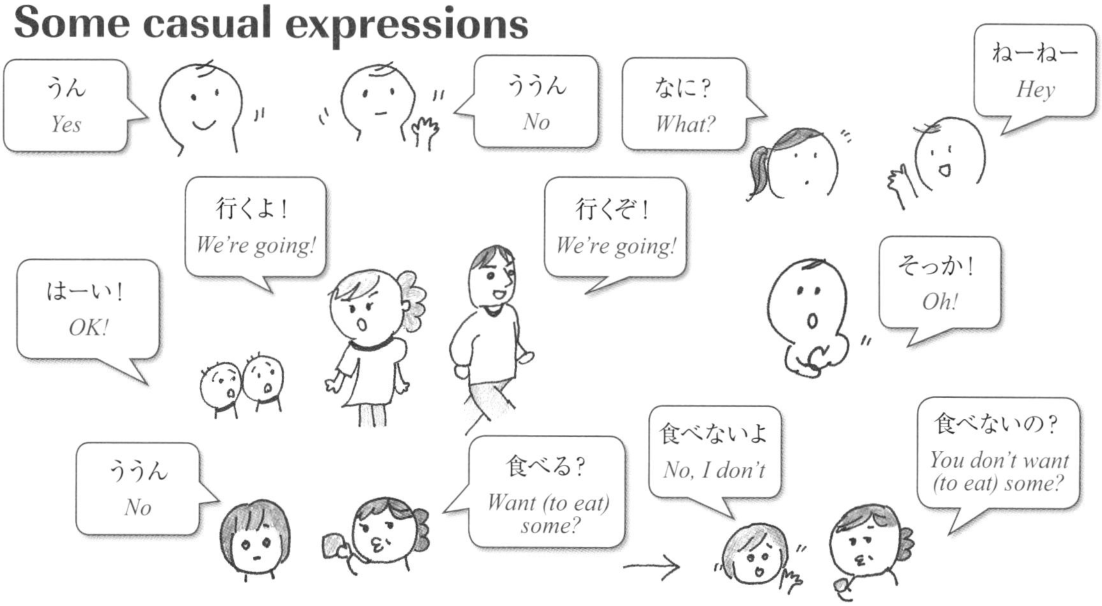

In English, the verb *want* is used in the above situations, but Japanese people generally don't use the words for want—ほしい or ～たい—when asking other people about their desires. In casual speech, you can just use the dictionary or nai-form of the verb as shown above (raising the pitch of the final syllable to indicate that it is a question).

Translation

Kana: Hey, do you wanna watch this?
Miki: Mmm…that's scary.
Kana: Oh. How about this one?
Miki: Nah, that's boring.
Kana: So which should we watch?
Miki: Umm...

新しい言葉 New Words

- □ねー hey
- □こっち this one; this way
- □つまんない boring (casual way to say つまらない)

Lesson 16 I like listening to music.

verb + の nominalization of the verb (turning it into a noun)

[dictionary form]

音楽を **聞く** のが好きです。

Ongaku o **kiku** no ga suki desu.

例 Ex. 日本語を話すのが苦手です。
Nihongo o hanasu no ga nigate desu.

いろんな人に会うのは楽しい。
Ironna hito ni au no wa tanoshii.

日本語を話すのは難しいです。
Nihongo o hanasu no wa muzukashii desu.

話すの	*speaking*
苦手	*not good at*
いろんな（いろいろな）	*various*
会うの	*meeting*

Point!

- 話すのが is pronounced as a single word with no pauses: hanasunoga.
- The particle that follows の depends on what comes next.
- Be careful not to confuse this usage with the present progressive (*-ing*) construction that uses て form:

食べています	→	I'm eating
食べるのが好きです	→	I like eating

Dialogue Tom and Yuka are talking about their hobbies.

トム： 趣味はなんですか？
ゆか： そうですね…料理を作るのが好きです。
トム： いいですね。僕は食べるのは好きだけど、作るのは苦手ですね。
ゆか： 私も食べるの大好きですよ。特に甘いもの。トムさんの趣味は？
トム： 僕はスポーツ見るのが好きなので、よくスポーツバーにいきます。

Tomu: Shumi wa nan desu ka?
Yuka: Sō desu ne…ryōri o tsukuru no ga suki desu.
Tomu: Ii desu ne. Boku wa taberu no wa suki da kedo, tsukuru no wa nigate desu ne.
Yuka: Watashi mo taberu no daisuki desu yo. Toku ni amaimono. Tomu-san no shumi wa?
Tomu: Boku wa supōtsu miru no ga suki nanode, yoku supōtsu-bā ni ikimasu.

Should I use が, は, or を after the の?

Let's consider を first since it is the easiest. を is only used when the verb nominalized by の is the direct object of another verb (a verb that expresses an action).

Examples of verbs that use を:

忘れる	聞く	見る	知る
wasureru	kiku	miru	shiru
to forget	*to hear*	*to see*	*to know*

牛乳を買うのを忘れました。
Gyūnyū o kau no o wasuremashita.
I forgot to buy milk.

ゆかさんが結婚するのを知りました。
Yuka-san ga kekkon suru no o shirimashita.
I knew that Yuka would marry.

But what if an action verb doesn't follow の? How do I choose between は and が?

This is a very tricky question, and arriving at the answer can take years of exposure to native usage. But don't despair! Words are typically used with either one or the other, so by memorizing the most commonly used expressions you can internalize the best choice for each situation naturally—which is how native Japanese speakers learn them anyway.

ギターを弾くのが得意です。
Gitā o hiku no ga tokui desu.
I'm good at playing guitar.

週末は起きるのが遅いです。
Shūmatsu wa okiru no ga osoi desu.
I wake up late on weekends.

Some adjectives that you will often see after は are たのしい, むずかしい, かんたん, たいへん, きもちいい, and よくない.

ひらがなを読むのは簡単です。
Hiragana o yomu no wa kantan desu.
Reading hiragana is easy.

海で泳ぐのは気持ちいいです。
Umi de oyogu no wa kimochi ii desu.
Swimming in the ocean feels nice.

Watch out!

When making comparisons between two things, use は.

ギターを弾くのは得意だけど、歌うのは苦手です。
Gitā o hiku no wa tokui dakedo, utau no wa nigate desu. *I'm pretty good at playing guitar, but not at singing.*

- Use も to indicate that the adjective applies to more than one action.

ひらがなを読むのも書くのも上手ですね。
Hiragana o yomu no mo kaku no mo jōzu desu ne. *You are good at both reading and writing hiragana.*

Translation

Tom: What are your hobbies?
Yuka: Well, I like cooking.
Tom: That's nice. I like to eat but I'm not good at cooking.
Yuka: I like to eat very much! Especially sweets. What's are your hobbies, Tom?
Tom: I like watching sports so I often go to sports bars.

新しい言葉 New Words

- ☐趣味 hobby
- ☐作るの making; cooking
- ☐特に especially, particularly
- ☐甘いもの sweets
- ☐スポーツバー sports bar

Lesson 17 Can I buy this item on display?

verb + ことができる can do 〈Verb〉

[dictionary form]

この展示品を **買う** ことができますか？

Kono tenjihin o **kau** koto ga dekimasu ka?

例 Ex. 電話を充電すること(が)できますか？
Denwa o jūden suru koto (ga) dekimasu ka?

カードで払うことができますか？
Kādo de harau koto ga dekimasu ka?

図書館で音楽を聞くことができません。
Toshokan de ongaku o kiku koto ga dekimasen.

展示品	*display item*
充電する	*to charge (batteries etc.)*
カード	*(credit) card*
図書館	*library*

Point!

- The verb and ことが are pronounced together as a single word.
- For verbs formed with する, the words することが are often omitted:
  充電することができます → 充電できます

Dialogue Mike is asking about snow monkeys at a tourist information desk.

マイク：スノーモンキーはどこでみることができますか？
ガイド：長野の地獄谷でみることができますよ。
マイク：その辺りで泊まることもできますか？
ガイド：はい、できますよ。
マイク：あと、車で行くことできますか？
ガイド：ええ、行けますよ。

Maiku: Sunō monkī wa doko de miru koto ga dekimasu ka?
Gaido: Nagano no Jigokudani de miru koto ga dekimasu yo.
Maiku: Sono atari de tomaru koto mo dekimasu ka?
Gaido: Hai, dekimasu yo.
Maiku: Ato, kuruma de iku koto dekimasu ka?
Gaido: Ē, ikemasu yo.

What's the difference?　行ける vs. 行くことができる

In *Practical Japanese 1*, we learned another way to create a verb's potential form.

行く	→	行ける		食べる	→	食べられる
iku		ikeru		taberu		taberareru.

These potential forms are more casual than ことができる and therefore you will encounter them more often.

Special verbs

見る and 聞く are special because they each have two potential forms. The first is used when you watch or listen to something intentionally, such as a movie or a song.

見られる
mirareru

聞ける
kikeru

このパソコンでテレビが見られます。
Kono pasokon de terebi ga miraremasu.
You can watch a TV show on this computer.

スマートフォンで好きな音楽が聞ける。
Sumāto-fon de sukina ongaku ga kikeru.
You can listen to your favorite music on your smartphone.

The second form is used when you happen to see or hear something around you.

見える
mieru

聞こえる
kikoeru

窓から空が見える。
Mado kara sora ga mieru.
I can see the sky from the window.

鳥の声が聞こえる。
Tori no koe ga kikoeru.
I can hear a bird singing.

Translation

Mike: Where can I see the snow monkeys?
Guide: You can see them at Jigokudani in Nagano.
Mike: Can I stay in lodging somewhere around there?
Guide: You can, yes.
Mike: Also, can I drive there?
Guide: Yes, you can get there by car.

新しい言葉　New Words

- □スノーモンキー　snow monkey
- □ガイド　(tourist) guide
- □泊まる　to stay (at a hotel etc.)
- □あと　also; one more thing

Lesson 18 Please don't park your car here.

～ないでください please don't ______

[nai-form]

ここに車を **止めない** でください。

Koko ni kuruma o **tomenai** de kudasai.

例 Ex. チケットを忘れないでください。
Chiketto o wasurenaide kudasai.

エスカレーターで走らないでください。
Esukarētā de hashiranaide kudasai.

この部屋に入らないでください。
Kono heya ni hairanaide kudasai.

止めない（とめる）	*to stop (something)*
エスカレーター	*escalator*
走らない（はしる）	*to run*
この部屋に	*into this room*
入らない（はいる）	*to enter*

Point!

- ない and で are pronounced as a single word.
- ないで by itself is informal—add ください to make it polite.

忘れないで	忘れないでください
don't forget	*please don't forget*

Dialogue A new employee is speaking to a coworker.

新人： 山田です。よろしくお願いします。
先輩： 鈴木です。よろしく。えーと、この部屋のルールを説明します。
ここで携帯を使わないでください。
食べ物も食べないで。
それからこのパソコンは使わないでください。いいですか。
新人： はい、わかりました。

Shinjin: Yamada desu. Yoroshiku onegai shimasu.
Senpai: Suzuki desu. Yoroshiku. Ēto, kono heya no rūru ni tsuite setsumei shimasu.
Koko de keitai o tsukawanaide kudasai.
Tabemono mo tabenaide.
Sorekara kono pasokon wa tsukawanaide kudasai. Ii desu ka?
Shinjin: Hai, wakarimashita.

Common expressions

押さないで
osanaide
don't push

話さないで
hanasanaide
don't talk

行かないで
ikanaide
don't go

見ないで
minaide
don't look

荷物を置かないで
nimotsu o okanaide
don't put belongings

写真を撮らないで
shashin o toranaide
don't take photographs

What's the difference? とめる vs. とまる

Transitive	Intransitive
The subject performs an action on the object. The particles は〜を are used: **Subject は Object を Verb**	There is no object for the action to affect. The particle が is used: **Subject が Verb**

私は車を止める。
Watashi wa kuruma o tomeru.
I will stop the car.

車が止まる。
Kuruma ga tomaru.
The car will stop.

彼女は窓を開ける。
Kanojo wa mado o akeru.
She opens the window.

電車のドアが開いた。
Densha no doa ga aita.
The train door opens.

先生はコップを落としました。
Sensei wa koppu o otoshimashita.
The teacher dropped the cup.

コップが落ちました。
Koppu ga ochimashita.
The cup dropped.

Translation

New Employee: I'm Yamada. Nice to meet you.

Senior Employee: I'm Suzuki. Nice to meet you, too. OK, I'll explain the rules for this room.
Please don't use your cellphone here.
Don't eat food here either.
Also, please don't use this computer. Got it?

New Employee: OK, I understand.

新しい言葉 New Words

- ☐新人 new employee
- ☐先輩 senior employee
- ☐ルール rules
- ☐説明する explan
- ☐携帯 cellphone

Lesson 19 I have to go now.

～ないといけません (formal) ～ないといけない (informal)

have to ________

[nai-form]

もう **行かない** といけません。

Mō ikanai to ikemasen.

例 Ex. もう帰らないといけません。
Mō kaeranai to ikemasen.

ここで降りないといけない。
Koko de orinai to ikenai.

ちゃんと言わないとだめ。
Chanto iwanai to dame.

もう	*already; soon; presently*
帰らない(かえる)	*to go back; to go home*
降りない(おりる)	*to get off*
ちゃんと	*properly; correctly*
言わない(いう)	*to say*

Point!

- と means *if* and いけません means *wrong, of no use, or it won't go well*. So 帰らないといけません literally means *if you don't go home, it won't go well*. But you can just think of the entire phrase ないといけません as an expression meaning *have to*.
- In casual conversation, native speakers often leave the いけない off and just say ～ないと (especially when speaking to themselves).

Dialogue Suzuki and Chris are at a festival venue.

鈴木： 最初に入場料を払わないといけませんよ。
クリス：入場料が必要ですか？
鈴木： ええ、そこでチケットを買わないと……
クリス：あ、人がたくさんいますね。並ばないといけない。
鈴木： うわーながく待たないといけませんね。どうしよう。
クリス：１時までに家に帰らないといけないから、無理ですよ。

Suzuki: Saisho ni nyūjōryō o harawanai to ikemasen yo.
Kurisu: Nyūjōryō ga hitsuyō desu ka?
Suzuki: Ē, soko de chiketto o kawanai to…
Kurisu: A, hito ga takusan imasu ne. Narabanai to ikenai.
Suzuki: Uwā—nagaku matanai to ikemasen ne. Dō shiyou.
Kurisu: Ichi-ji made ni uchi ni kaeranai to ikenai kara, muri desu yo.

Other expressions

Japanese has some other expressions that are very similar to ～ないといけない.

なければなりません
nakereba narimasen

This sounds quite severe and is used for rules, responsibilities, and duties.

規則を作らなければなりません。
Kisoku o tsukuranakereba narimasen.
We must create some rules.

ないといけません **なきゃいけません**
nai to ikemasen **nakya ikemasen**

These two interchangeable expressions indicate the things you need to do.

行かないといけません。
Ikanai to ikemasen.
I need to go.

行かなきゃ…
Ikanakya…
I gotta go...

なきゃ だめ **なくちゃだめ**
nakya dame **nakucha dame**

Use these casual expressions when talking to children or friends—they are similar to commands, just not quite as strong.

手あらわなきゃだめ!
Te arawanakya dame!
Be sure to wash your hands!

え～だめ?
Ē... dame?
Aww, do I have to?

What's the difference? までに vs. まで

When by itself, まで means until. But when に follows まで, it indicates a stopping point in time (like a deadline).

５時までに、この本を読み終わらなきゃいけません。
Go-ji made ni, kono hon o yomiowaranakya ikemasen.
I have to finish reading this book by 5 o'clock.

５時まで、この本を読みます。
Go-ji made, kono hon o yomimasu.
I will read this book until 5 o'clock.

Translation

Suzuki: First, we have to pay the entry fee.
Chris: An entry fee is required?
Suzuki: Yes, we have to buy the tickets there...
Chris: Oh, there's a lot of people. We have to get in line.
Suzuki: Wow—we will have to wait for a long time. What should we do?
Chris: I have to be home by one o'clock, so it's impossible.

新しい言葉 New Words

- □最初に (at) first
- □入場料 entry fee
- □払わない（はらう） to pay
- □必要 need; requirement
- □並ばない（ならぶ） to get in line
- □までに by (time, date)
- □無理 impossible

Lesson 20 You don't need to apologize.

～なくてもいい don't have to ________ no need to ________

[nai-form > nakutemo]

謝らなくても いいですよ。

Ayamaranakute mo ii desu yo.

薬	*medicine*
持ってこなくて（もってくる）	*to bring*
お弁当	*boxed lunch*

例 Ex. 漢字で書かなくてもいいです。
Kanji de kakanakute mo ii desu.

この薬は毎日飲まなくてもいいですか。
Kono kusuri wa mainichi nomanakute mo ii desu ka.

学校にお弁当を持ってこなくてもいいです。
Gakkō ni o-bentō o motte konakute mo ii desu.

Point!

- To form this expression, change the ない ending to なくて then add も and いい.

書かない → 書かなくて + も + いい → 書かなくてもいい

don't write → *don't have to write*

Dialogue

Jayson is eating with his Japanese mother-in-law.

義理の母：	納豆食べますか？	**Giri no haha:**	Natto tabemasu ka?
ジェイソン：	うー…	**Jeison:**	Ū…
義理の母：	無理して食べなくてもいいですよ。	**Giri no haha:**	Muri shite tabenakutemo ii desu yo.
ジェイソン：	すみません。	**Jeison:**	Sumimasen.
義理の母：	謝らなくてもいいですよ。	**Giri no haha:**	Ayamaranakute mo ii desu yo.
ジェイソン：	じゃ、全部食べなくてもいいですか？	**Jeison:**	Ja, zenbu tabenakute mo ii desu ka?

Common expressions

食べ物をしばらく買わなくてもいい。
Tabemono o shibaraku kawanakute mo ii.
I don't have to buy groceries for a while.

学校も会社も行かなくてもいい。
Gakkō mo kaisha mo ikanakute mo ii.
We don't need to go to school or work.

そんなに心配しなくてもいい。
Sonna ni shinpai shinakute mo ii.
You don't have to worry so much.

わざわざ来なくてもいい。
Wazawaza konakute mo ii.
You don't need to come all the way here.

ハンコを押さなくてもいいです。
Hanko o osanakute mo ii desu.
You don't need to stamp your seal.

Sometimes you can use other words in place of いい:

予約しなくても大丈夫だよ。
Yoyaku shinakute mo daijōbu da yo.
You don't have to make a reservation.

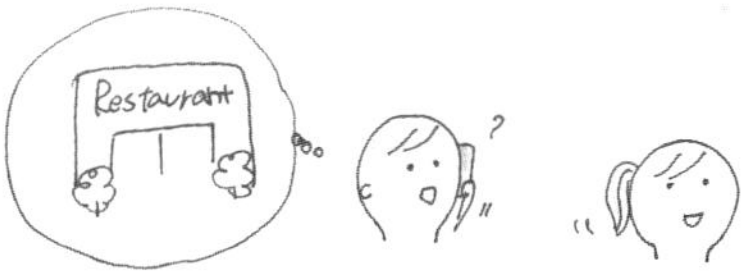

What's the difference?　なくてもいい vs. 必要がない

食べなくてもいいです。
Tabenakute mo ii desu.
You don't have to eat.

食べる必要がないです。
Taberu hitsuyō ga nai desu.
Eating is not necessary.

As you can see from the English translations, these expressions say essentially the same thing. The distinction comes down to usage: 必要がない is used more in writing, while なくてもいい appears more often in daily conversation.

There is a special usage of しなくても (without the いい) that is equivalent to saying "You shouldn't have..." when someone gives you a present or does you a favor.

そんなことしなくても…
Sonna koto shinakute mo...
You shouldn't have...

Translation

Mother-in-law: Want some *natto*?
Jayson: Uhh...
Mother-in-law: You don't have to force yourself to eat it.
Jayson: Sorry...
Mother-in-law: No need to apologize.
Jayson: Well…I don't have to eat it all, do I?

新しい言葉 New Words

☐納豆　fermented soybeans
☐無理して　to push yourself
☐謝らなくて (あやまる)　to apologize
☐全部　all

Lesson 21 You shouldn't buy that.

ない form + ほうがいい shouldn't ________ had better not ________

[nai-form]

それは **買わない** ほうがいいですよ。

Sore wa kawanai hō ga ii desu yo.

被災地	*disaster area*
危ない	*dangerous*
高価なもの	*expensive thing*

例 Ex. お酒をあまり飲まないほうがいいですよ。
O-sake o amari nomanai hō ga ii desu yo.

被災地は危ないから、行かないほうがいいでしょう。
Hisaichi wa abunai kara, ikanai hō ga ii deshou.

高価なものを買わないほうがよかったです。
Kōkanamono o kawanai hō ga yokatta desu.

Point!

- ないほうがいいです（よ）is used when giving advice.
- ないほうがよかった shows the speaker's regret.
- For affirmative sentences, the past tense (ta-form) is used. See p. 94.

Dialogue Joan has a rash and is looking for a cream at the drugstore.

薬剤師：	どうしましたか？	**Yakuzaishi:**	Dō shimashita ka?
ジョーン：	昨日から腕がかゆいんです。	**Jōn:**	Kinou kara ude ga kayui n desu.
薬剤師：	触らないほうがいいですよ。	**Yakuzaishi:**	Sawaranai hō ga ii desu yo.
ジョーン：	そうですね。でもとてもかゆくて……	**Jōn:**	Sō desu ne. Demo totemo kayukute…
薬剤師：	かゆくても、掻かないほうがいいです。	**Yakuzaishi:**	Kayukutemo, kakanai hō ga ii desu.
ジョーン：	この薬は効きますか？	**Jōn:**	Kono kusuri wa kikimasu ka?
薬剤師：	それは強いから塗らないほうがいいですね。こっちをどうぞ。	**Yakuzaishi:**	Sore wa tsuyoi kara nuranai hō ga ii desu ne. Kocchi o dōzo.

Common expressions

のどが痛い…
Nodo ga itai...
My throat hurts...

あまり話さないほうがいいですよ。
Amari hanasanai hō ga ii desu yo.
You had better not talk much.

明日は雨ですね。
Ashita wa ame desu ne.
It'll rain tomorrow.

山に行かないほうがいいでしょうね。
Yama ni ikanai hō ga ii deshou ne.
We shouldn't go to the mountain, I guess.

つかれた…
Tsukareta…
I'm tired...

無理しないほうがいいよ。
Muri shinai hō ga ii yo.
You shouldn't overdo it.

To show regret:

今日の映画は恐かった…見ないほうがよかった。
Kyou no eiga wa kowakatta…minai hō ga yokatta.
Today's movie was scary...I shouldn't have watched it.

What's the difference? ないほうがよかった vs. なければよかった

食べないほうがよかった。
Tabenai hō ga yokatta.
I shouldn't have eaten that.

食べなければよかった！
Tabenakereba yokatta!
Eating that was such a mistake!

There isn't massive difference between these two expressions—it's mostly a matter of degree. ほうがいい simply compares the opposing actions of 食べる and 食べない, while 食べなければよかった indicates a hypothetical situation and suggests that the speaker more strongly regrets the outcome.

Translation

Pharmacist: What's wrong?
Joan: My arm has been itchy since yesterday.
Pharmacist: You shouldn't touch it.
Joan: I know. But it's very itchy...
Pharmacist: Even if it's itchy, you shouldn't scratch it.
Joan: Is this cream effective?
Pharmacist: That's strong, so you'd better not use it. Use this one.

新しい言葉 New Words

- □薬剤師 pharmacist
- □腕 arm
- □かゆい itchy
- □掻かない（かく） to scratch
- □効きます（きく） to be effective
- □強い strong
- □塗らない（ぬる） to apply (cream, paint, etc.)

Lesson 22 I decided to go back to my hometown.

ことにする decide to ________

[dictionary nai-form]

田舎に 帰る ことにしました。

Inaka ni kaeru koto ni shimashita.

例 Ex. 甘いものを食べないことにしました。
Amai mono o tabenai koto ni shimashita.

毎日1時間運動することにしました。
Mainichi ichi-jikan undō suru koto ni shimashita.

社長は会議を開くことにしました。
Shachō wa kaigi o hiraku koto ni shimashita.

ことにしました	*decided to*
甘いもの	*sweets*
運動する	*to exercise*
社長	*CEO*
会議	*conference*
開く	*to hold (a meeting or event)*

Point!

- Literally, こと means *thing* and します means *to do.*
- The particle に always comes before しました.

Dialogue Aoki is talking to his coworker about a decision he has made.

青木：	いろいろ考えましたけど、会社をやめることにしました。	**Aoki:**	Iroiro kangaemashita kedo, kaisha o yameru koto ni shimashita.
浅野：	そう…で、やめて何することにしたんですか。	**Asano:**	Sō…de, yamete nani suru koto ni shita n desu ka.
青木：	田舎に帰ることにしました。 実家は農家なので、一緒に農業することにしたんです。 親ももう年だし……	**Aoki:**	Inaka ni kaeru koto ni shimashita. Jikka wa nōka nanode, issho ni nōgyō suru koto ni shita n desu. Oya mo mō toshi da shi…
浅野：	そうですか。寂しくなるけど頑張ってください。	**Asano:**	Sō desu ka. Sabishiku naru kedo ganbatte kudasai.

Common expressions

あれ、今日は飲まないの？
Are, kyou wa nomanai no?
Hey, you aren't drinking today?

調子が悪いから、しばらくお酒は飲まないことにした。
Chōshi ga warui kara, shibaraku o-sake wa nomanai koto ni shita.
I don't feel well, so I've decided not to drink alcohol for a bit.

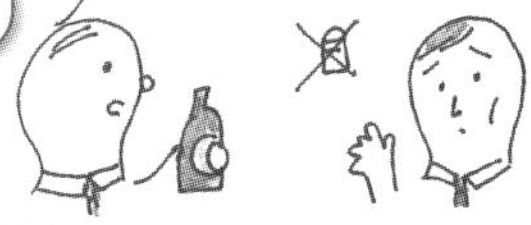

日本語だけで話すことになりました…
Nihongo dake de hanasu koto ni narimashita...
It's been decided that we will only speak in Japanese...

これからは、英語を話さないことにしましょう。
Korekara wa, eigo o hanasanai koto ni shimashou.
Let's agree to not speak English from here on out.

What's the difference? ことにする vs. ことになる

Like ことにする, the phrase ことになる is used to indicate that a decision has been made. The difference is that ことになる implies the decision wasn't entirely your own, so it can be used even when you had no part in making the decision and want to express that the decision is not really your fault or intention.

仕事で東京に引っ越すことになりました。
Shigoto de Tōkyō ni sumu koto ni narimashita.
It's been decided that I have to move Tokyo for my job.

祭りをしないことになりました。
Matsuri o shinai koto ni narimashita.
We've decided to cancel the festival.

週末、試合をすることになりました。
Shūmatsu, shiai o suru koto ni narimashita.
They've decided to have a scrimmage this weekend.

- ことになりました is used with decisions that inherently involve other people (events, matches, etc.).

One more thing

When you order food, use にする instead of ことにする:

何にする？
Nan ni suru?
What are you getting?

うーん、どうしよう。
Ūn, dō shiyou.
Hmm, let's see..

じゃ、ピザにする。
Ja, piza ni suru.
I'll have the pizza.

Translation

Aoki: After giving it a lot of thought, I decided to quit my job here.

Asano: Oh…well, what are you going to do?

Aoki: I've decided to go back to my hometown. My parents are farmers, so I'm going to work on the farm with them.
They are already getting old...

Asano: I see. You'll be missed, but I wish you luck.

新しい言葉 New Words

- □考えた（かんがえる） to think
- □実家 parents' house
- □農家 farmer
- □農業 farming; agriculture
- □もう年 getting old (people and animals)

てけい te-form

The te-form of a verb is used for a variety of purposes, including making requests (～てください), asking for permission (～てもいいですか), connecting verbs and clauses (～て～て and ～てから), and expressing state of being (～ています).

Group 1 verbs conjugate to te-form according to the final character of their dictionary forms:

う	becomes	って	→	かう	to	かって
つ	becomes	って	→	まつ	to	まって
る	becomes	って	→	とる	to	とって
ぬ	becomes	んで	→	しぬ	to	しんで
ぶ	becomes	んで	→	あそぶ	to	あそんで
む	becomes	んで	→	のむ	to	のんで
く	becomes	いて	→	かく	to	かいて
ぐ	becomes	いで	→	いそぐ	to	いそいで
す	becomes	して	→	はなす	to	はなして

Watch out! The verb 行く has an irregular te-form: 行って.

Group 1

	dictionary form		te-form	
to meet	会う	au	会って	atte
to sing	歌う	utau	歌って	utatte
to buy	買う	kau	買って	katte
to say	言う	iu	言って	itte
to differ	違う	chigau	違って	chigatte
to pay	払う	harau	払って	haratte
to use	使う	tsukau	使って	tsukatte
to hold	持つ	motsu	持って	motte
to wait	待つ	matsu	待って	matte
to stand	立つ	tatsu	立って	tatte
to take	取る	toru	取って	totte
to enter	入る	hairu	入って	haitte
to make	作る	tsukuru	作って	tsukutte
to send	送る	okuru	送って	okutte
to know	知る	shiru	知って	shitte
to ride	乗る	noru	乗って	notte
to cut	切る	kiru	切って	kitte
to be troubled	困る	komaru	困って	komatte
to return	帰る	kaeru	帰って	kaette
to climb	登る	noboru	登って	nobotte
to sleep	眠る	nemuru	眠って	nemutte
to choose	選ぶ	erabu	選んで	erande

to carry	運ぶ	hakobu	運んで	hakonde
to call	呼ぶ	yobu	呼んで	yonde
to fall	転ぶ	korobu	転んで	koronde
to live	住む	sumu	住んで	sunde
to be crowded	混む	komu	混んで	konde
to read	読む	yomu	読んで	yonde
to rest	休む	yasumu	休んで	yasunde
to write	書く	kaku	書いて	kaite
to arrive	着く	tsuku	着いて	tsuite
to hear/listen/ask	聞く	kiku	聞いて	kiite
to walk	歩く	aruku	歩いて	aruite
to swim	泳ぐ	oyogu	泳いで	oyoide
to hurry	急ぐ	isogu	急いで	isoide
to hand or pass	渡す	watasu	渡して	watashite
to lend or rent	貸す	kasu	貸して	kashite
to give back	返す	kaesu	返して	kaeshite
to look for	探す	sagasu	探して	sagashite
to talk or speak	話す	hanasu	話して	hanashite

Group 2

	dictionary form		te-form	
to wake	起きる	okiru	起きて	okite
to sleep	寝る	neru	寝て	nete
to open	開ける	akeru	開けて	akete
to close	閉める	shimeru	閉めて	shimete
to put in	入れる	ireru	入れて	irete
to see/look/watch	見る	miru	見て	mite
to teach	教える	oshieru	教えて	oshiete
to show	見せる	miseru	見せて	misete
to stop	止める	tomeru	止めて	tomete
to forget	忘れる	wasureru	忘れて	wasurete
to wear	着る	kiru	着て	kite

Group 3

	dictionary form		te-form	
to do	する	suru	して	shite
to come	来る	kuru	来て	kite

Lesson 23 I wake up in the morning then drink some coffee.

[te-form]

朝 起きて コーヒーを 飲みます。

Asa okite kōhī o nomimasu.

秋葉原	*a famous place in Tokyo*
遅い	*late at night*
お寺	*temple*
それから	*and then*

例 Ex. 昨日は秋葉原に行って買い物しました。
Kinou wa Akihabara ni itte kaimono shimashita.

夜遅いので、家に帰って寝ます。
Yoruosoi node, uchi ni kaette nemasu.

最初に京都に行ってお寺を見て、それから大阪に行って友達に会いました。
Saisho ni Kyōto ni itte o-tera o mite, sorekara Ōsaka ni itte tomodachi ni aimashita.

Point!

- This usage of te-form connects verbs; to connect nouns, use と.
- You can use te-form more than once in the same sentence.
- The tense (past, present, etc.) is indicated by the verb at the end of sentence.
- The actions of verbs connected using te-form occur in chronological order.

Dialogue A teacher and students are interacting at a cooking class.

先生： さて、今日はカレーライスを作りますよ。
はじめに、野菜をあらって、一口大にきってください。
それから、なべに油を入れて熱して肉と野菜をいためてください。
そこに水を入れて、煮て、それから……

生徒： 先生、ルーも入れますか？

先生： いえいえ、ルーは10分くらい煮てから入れてくださいね。

Sensei: Sate, kyou wa karē-raisu o tsukurimasu yo.
Hajime ni, yasai o aratte, hitokuchidai ni kitte kudasai.
Sorekara, nabe ni abura o irete nesshite niku to yasai o itamete kudasai.
Soko ni mizu o irete, nite, sorekara…

Seito: Sensei, rū mo iremasu ka?

Sensei: Ie ie, rū wa juppun kurai nite kara irete kudasai ne.

What's the difference? て vs. てから

In general, actions connected with te-form occur in the same order that they appear in the sentence. When から follows the te-form of a verb, it simply emphasizes that the action of the verb in te-form must take place before the action of the verb that follows. For that reason, てから appears often in instructions, rules, and requirements.

歯をみがいて寝ます。
Ha o migaite nemasu.
I'll brush my teeth then go to sleep.

歯をみがいてから、寝ます。
Ha o migaite kara, nemasu.
I'll brush my teeth before going to sleep.

ノックをして部屋に入りました。
Nokku o shite heya ni hairimashita.
I knocked and entered the room.

ノックをしてから入ってください。
Nokku o shite kara haitte kudasai.
Please knock before entering.

宿題をして、友達と遊びます。
Shukudai o shite, tomodachi to asobimasu.
I'll do my homework then hang out with my friend.

宿題が終わってから、友達と遊びます。
Shukudai ga owatte kara, tomodachi to asobimasu.
I'll finish my homework before hanging out with my friend.

Watch out!

When から is used with verb forms other than te-form, it means *because* or *so*.

そろそろご飯を食べるから、
お菓子は食べないほうがいい。
Sorosoro gohan o taberu kara, okashi wa tabenai hō ga ii.
We'll eat dinner soon, so you shouldn't eat any snacks.

彼は仕事してるから、電話にでられません。
Kare wa shigoto shiteru kara, denwa ni deraremasen.
He's working, so he can't answer the phone.

Cooking words 料理の言葉

切る
kiru
to cut

入れる
ireru
to add

熱する
nessuru
to heat

炒める
itameru
to fry

盛る
moru
to serve

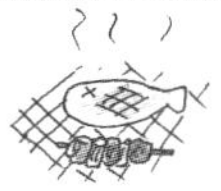
焼く
yaku
to grill

ごはんをとぐ
gohan o togu
to rinse rice

ごはんをたく
gohan o taku
to cook rice

ゆでる
yuderu
to boil in water

にる
niru
to simmer

出来上がり
dekiagari
finished

Translation

Teacher: Now then, today we are going to cook curry and rice.
First, wash the vegetables and cut them into bite-sized pieces.
Then put the oil into the pan, heat it up, and sauté the meat and vegetables.

Student: Teacher, should we add the roux too?

Teacher: No, after boiling for ten minutes you can add the roux.

新しい言葉 New Words

- ☐カレーライス curry and rice
- ☐野菜 vegetable
- ☐一口大 bite-size pieces
- ☐なべ pot
- ☐ルー roux
- ☐それから (and) then

Lesson 24 I'm heading there now.

[te-form]

今 **向かって** います。

Ima mukatte imasu.

向かっています(むかう)
heading somewhere
あとで *later*
何をしていましたか？
What were you doing?

例 Ex. 父は今寝ています。
Chichi wa ima nete imasu.

今、仕事してるので、あとで電話します。
Ima, shigoto shiteru node, ato de denwa shimasu.

昨日の１２時ごろ何をしてましたか？
Kinou no jūni-ji goro nani o shitemashita ka?

Point!

- When you add います to the te-form of an action verb, it indicates that the action is currently ongoing.
- ていました is used for actions that were ongoing at some point in the past but have since stopped (the "past progressive").
- In conversation, ～ています and ～ていました are usually shortened to ～てます and ～てました.

Dialogue Aoki is working in his office when he receives a phone call from his boss.

部長： もしもし、青木？ 今何してる？
青木： あ、部長。お疲れ様です。今、出張の報告書を書いてますけど……
部長： それはあとででいいから、すぐ会議室に来て。
３時の会議の準備、手伝って。
青木： わかりました。すぐ行きます。

Buchō: Moshimoshi, Aoki? Ima nani shiteru?
Aoki: A, Buchō, otsukaresama desu. Ima, shuccho no hōkokusho o kaitemasu kedo…
Buchō: Sore atode de ii kara, sugu kaigishitsu ni kite.
San-ji no kaigi no junbi, tetsudatte.
Aoki: Wakarimashita. Sugu ikimasu.

Using している

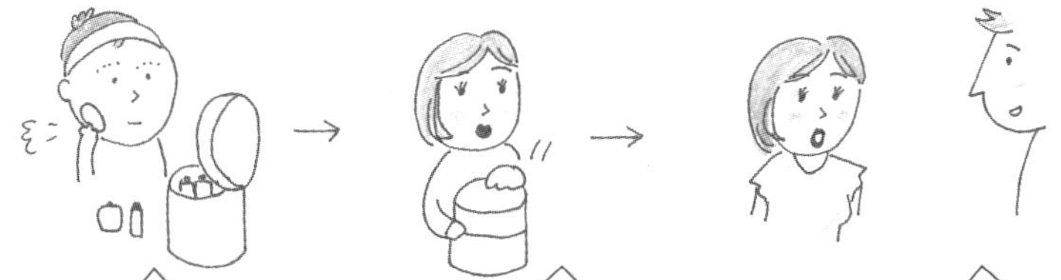

This usage of しています is introduced on the page 76.

化粧しています keshō shite imasu *applying makeup*	化粧しました keshō shimashita *applied makeup*	化粧しています keshō shite imasu *wearing makeup*

Since ています can indicate either a continuous state or a continuous activity that is presently taking place, it is quite often used with a time (毎日, ずっと, 今, etc.) or some other word that helps clarify its meaning, such as a location.

今、野菜ジュースを飲んでいます。
Ima, yasai jūsu o nonde imasu.
I am drinking vegetable juice right now.

毎日、野菜ジュースを飲んでいます。
Mainichi, yasai jūsu o nonde imasu.
I drink vegetable juice every day.

今、図書館で日本語を勉強しています。
Ima, toshokan de nihongo o benkyō shite imasu.
I'm studying Japanese in the library now.

ずっと日本語を勉強しています。
Zutto nihongo o benkyō shite imasu.
I've been studying Japanese for a long time.

What's the difference? しました vs. していました

Since していました is used to indicate that an action took place during a specific time interval, it is often paired with a time word or with another action or event that occurred at the same time.

昨日、勉強しました。
Kinou, benkyō shimashita.
I studied yesterday.

昨日の2時ごろ、勉強していました。
Kinou no ni-ji goro, benkyō shite imashita.
Around two o'clock yesterday, I was studying.

Also note that ～ている cannot be used with momentary actions because it implies a continuous action.

授業中に、寝ていました。
Jugyō-chū ni, nete imashita.
I was sleeping during class.

授業中に、消しゴムを落としました。
Jugyō-chū ni keshigomu o otoshimashita.
I dropped my eraser during class.

Translation

Manager: Hello, Aoki? What are you doing now?

Aoki: I'm writing a report about my business trip.

Manager: You can do that later. Come to the meeting room now.
Help me prepare for the meeting that starts at three o'clock.

Aoki: OK. I'll come right away.

新しい言葉 New Words

- □お疲れさまです used to start conversations with coworkers during work
- □出張 business trip
- □あとで later
- □でいい OK with
- □会議室 meeting room
- □準備 preparation

Lesson 25 I live in Tokyo.

[te-form]

東京に **住んで** います。

Tōkyō ni **sunde** imasu.

住んでいます(すむ) *to live*
働いています(はたらく) *to work*
結婚しています(けっこんする) *to marry*
退職して(たいしょくする) *to retire*
のんびり *relaxingly*
過ごしています(すごす) *to spend time*

例 Ex. 日本の会社で働いています。
Nihon no kaisha de hataraite imasu.

兄は結婚しています。
Ani wa kekkon shite imasu.

父は退職して家でのんびり過ごしています。
Chichi wa taishoku shite uchi de nonbiri sugoshite imasu.

Point!

- This ています expresses a continuous state, such as living, being married, working, commuting, or spending time. English sometimes uses adjectives to do this, for example in the statement *I am married*; in Japanese, however, you can't say **私は結婚です**—you must use **結婚しています**.

Self-introduction Jikoshōkai

はじめまして。マイクと申します。よろしくお願いします。	Hajimemashite. Maiku to mōshimasu. Yoroshiku onegai shimasu.
2年前にアメリカのミシシッピから来ました。	Ni-nen mae ni amerika no mishishippi kara kimashita.
今は、妻と子供と一緒に横浜に住んでます。	Ima wa tsuma to kodomo to issho ni Yokohama ni sundemasu.
子供は横浜でインターナショナルスクールに通っています。	Kodomo wa Yokohama de intānashonaru sukūru ni kayottemasu.
わたしは日本の会社につとめています。	Watashi wa nihon no kaisha ni tsutometemasu.
妻は英語教師で、うちの近くの英会話学校で教えてます。	Tsuma wa eigo-kyōshi de, uchi no chikaku no eikaiwa gakkō de oshietemasu.

What's the difference? 通います vs. 通っています

子供は学校に通います。 Kodomo wa gakkō ni kayoimasu.	**General statement:** *Children attend school.*
4月から学校に通います。 Shi-gatsu kara gakkō ni kayoimasu.	**Future tense:** *I'll attend school starting in April.*
料理学校に通っています。 Ryōri gakkō ni kayotte imasu.	**Continuous state:** *I'm attending a culinary school.*

Life Events

生まれる
umareru
to be born

入学する
nyūgaku suru
to enter school

学校に通う
gakkō ni kayou
to go (commute) to school

卒業する
sotsugyō suru
to graduate

就職する
shūshoku suru
to get a job

結婚する
kekkon suru
to get married

子供ができる
kodomo ga dekiru
to have a child

転職する
tenshoku suru
to change jobs

引っ越す
hikkosu
to move

離婚する
rikon suru
to get divorced

再婚する
saikon suru
to remarry

退職する
taishoku suru
to retire

老後を楽しむ
rōgo o tanoshimu
to enjoy one's golden years

死ぬ・亡くなる
shinu / nakunaru
to die / to pass away

Translation

Hello, I'm Mike. Nice to meet you.
Two years ago I came here from Mississippi.
I live in Yokohama with my wife and child.
My child goes to an international school in Yokohama.
I work for a Japanese company.
My wife is an English teacher; she teaches at an English-conversation school near our house.

新しい言葉 New Words

- □申します (honorific form of いう) to say
- □インターナショナルスクール international school
- □つとめてます（～につとめる） work for
- □英語教師 English teacher
- □英語会話 English conversation

Lesson 26 He is skinny.

[te-form]

彼は **やせて** います。

Kare wa **yasete** imasu.

例 Ex. うちのネコは太ってます。
Uchi no neko wa futottemasu.

父は眼鏡をかけています。
Chichi wa megane o kakete imasu.

彼女は結婚指輪をしています。
Kanojo wa kekkon yubiwa o shite imasu.

やせています (やせる)	*to be skinny* *lose weight*
うちの	*our; my*
太っています (ふとる)	*to be fat* *gain weight*
眼鏡	*glasses*
結婚指輪	*wedding ring*

Point!

- This ています is similar to the one introduced in the previous lesson for describing continuous states of activity, except it is used to describe people or things.
- かけています is used for wearing with glasses, but other articles of clothing use different verbs.

Dialogue Jennifer is an international student talking to her classmate, Yūka.

ジェニファー：日本人ってみんなやせてるね。
ゆうか：え～そうかな……
ジェニファー：そうだよ。それに、みんな制服着て短いスカートはいてるね。
アメリカの女の子は、たいていジーンズをはいてるよ。こういう……
ゆうか：あっ、ジェニー、チャック開いてるよ！
ジェニファー：恥ずかしい！

Jenifā: Nihonjin tte minna yaseteru ne.
Yūka: Ē—sō ka na...
Jenifā: Sō da yo. Sore ni, minna seifuku kite mijikai sukāto haiteru ne.
Amerika no onnanoko wa taitei jīnzu o haiteiru yo. Kō iu...
Yūka: A, Jenī, chakku aiteru yo!
Jenifā: Hazukashii!

Describing people with ています

やせている
yasete iru

太っている
futotte iru

スカーフ
sukāfu
マフラー を巻いている
mafurā o maite iru

手袋
tebukuro
をしている
o shite iru

シャツ
shatsu
ジャケットを着ている
jaketto o kite iru

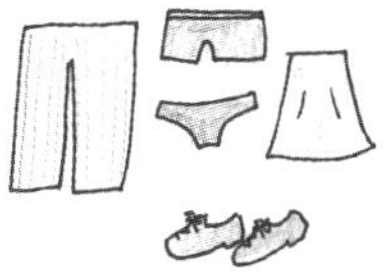

ズボン
zubon
スカートをはいている
sukāto o haite iru

メガネをかけている
megane o kakete iru

アクセサリーをつけている
aksesarī o tsukete iru

帽子をかぶっている
bōshi o kabutte iru

荷物
nimotsu
バッグを持っている
baggu o motte iru

Chapter 2

Describing a state with が〜ている

お店が開いている
o-mise ga aite iru

お店が閉まっている
o-mise ga shimatte iru

テレビが壊れている
terebi ga kowarete iru

葉っぱが落ちている
happa ga ochite iru

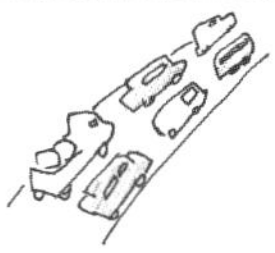

道が混んでいる
michi ga konde iru

電車が空いている
densha ga suite iru

電気がついている
denki ga tsuite iru

電気が消えている
denki ga kiete iru

コップが割れている
koppu ga warete iru

車が止まっている
kuruma ga tomatte iru

Translation

Jennifer: All Japanese people are skinny, aren't they.
Yūka: Um, I dunno about that...
Jennifer: It's true! Plus, everyone wears a school uniform with a short skirt.
Girls in America usually wear jeans. Like this....
Yūka: Oh, Jenny, your zipper is open!
Jennifer: I'm so embarrassed!

新しい言葉 New Words

- □制服 uniform
- □短い short
- □チャック zipper
- □開いてる(あく) open
- □恥ずかしい embarrassed

Lesson 27 I'll go ahead and make a reservation.

[te-form]

予約して Yoyaku shite	おきます。 okimasu.

例 Ex. インターネットで調べておきました。
Intānetto de shirabete okimashita.

友達が来るので部屋を掃除しておきます。
Tomodachi ga kuru node heya o sōji shite okimasu.

忘れるから、紙に書いといて。
Wasureru kara, kami ni kaitoite.

予約 *reservation*
インターネット *the Internet*
調べて(しらべる) *to research or look up*
掃除して(そうじする) *to clean*
忘れる(わすれる) *to forget*

Point!

- When おく follows the te-form of a verb, it implies that the verb's action is being done in advance of another activity or so that it doesn't have to be done or worried about later. In English, this is often expressed using "go ahead and *<verb>*."
- You don't have to specify the reason for doing the action when using ておく. For example, if someone says 部屋を掃除しておきます, you can assume that there is a specific reason why they are cleaning the room—perhaps a friend will be visiting soon.
- ～ておく can be shortened to ～とく in casual Japanese, similar to how ～ている can become ～てる.

Dialogue A couple is preparing for their trip.

彼女：明日はいよいよハワイ旅行だね。楽しみ～
彼氏：うん、もうホテルも予約しておいたし、飛行機のチケットもとっといたし。
彼女：そうだね。あっ、日焼け止め買っといた？
彼氏：うん、買っといた。俺のバッグにいれといたよ。

Kanojo: Ashita wa iyoiyo Hawai ryokō dane. Tanoshimi~
Kareshi: Un, mō hoteru mo yoyaku shite oita shi, hikōki no chiketto mo tottoita shi.
Kanojo: Sō da ne. A, hiyakedome kattoita?
Kareshi: Un, kattoita. Ore no baggu ni iretoita yo.

You can attach でおく to the ない form of a verb to get the same effect:

彼女が怒るから言わないでおく。
Kanojo ga okoru kara iwanaide oku. *My girlfriend will get angry so I won't say it.*

Sometimes, ～ておく indicates that the action is done to prevent something bad from happening:

台風が来るから、練習をやめとく。
Taifū ga kuru kara, renshū o yametoku.
Since there's a typhoon coming, we'll go ahead and cancel practice.

What's the difference? ～ている vs. ～ておく vs. ～てある

先生が黒板に書いている。
Sensei wa kokuban ni kaite iru.
The teacher is writing on the chalkboard.

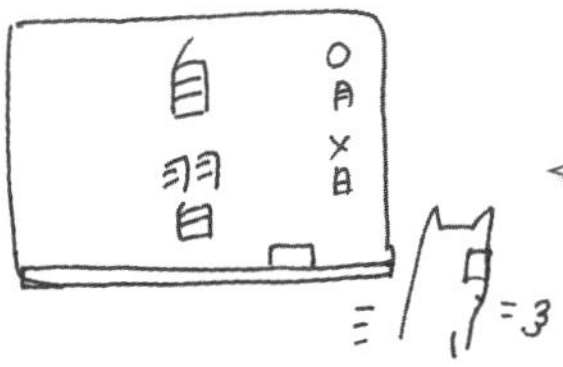

先生が黒板に書いておいた。
Sensei ga kokuban ni kaite oita.
The teacher went ahead and wrote on the chalkboard.

何かが黒板に書いてある。
Nanika ga kokuban ni kaite aru.
Something is written on the chalkboard.

It's confusing…

Just remember that ～てある is used when the actor is unknown or not important.

Translation

Girlfriend: Our Hawaii trip finally starts tomorrow! I'm excited~

Boyfriend: Yeah, we already booked a hotel room and got plane tickets.

Girlfriend: That's right. Oh, did you buy some sunscreen?

Boyfriend: Yep, I went ahead and bought some and put it in my bag.

新しい言葉 New Words

- □いよいよ finally
- □楽しみ exciting
- □飛行機 airplane
- □とっといた(とる) to take or get
- □日焼け止め sunscreen
- □入れといた(いれる) to put in

Lesson 28 I lost my wallet.

[te-form]

財布を **失くして** しまいました。

Saifu o **nakushite** shimaimashita.

例 Ex. 犬が死んでしまいました。
Inu ga shinde shimaimashita.

ヘッドセットこわしちゃった。
Heddsetto kowashichatta.

飲んじゃった。
Nonjatta.

失くして(なくす)	*to lose*
寝坊して(ねぼうする)	*overslept*
怒って(おこる)	*to get upset*

Point!

- Adding しまいます (or its casual form しまう) to the te-form of a verb indicates regret or sadness. It can also be used to show that the action of the verb is completed.
- In casual Japanese, this expression is often shortened. For verbs whose te-form ends in て, it becomes ちゃう; for those that end in で, it becomes じゃう.

してしまう → しちゃう	飲んでしまう → 飲んじゃう
してしまった → しちゃった	飲んでしまった → 飲んじゃった

Dialogue Ryōsuke is running late for school.

亮介：あっ、ヤバイ！ 寝坊しちゃった。
電車行っちゃったかな……

学校に着いたあと…

亮介：すみません、電車に乗り遅れてしまいました。

教師：またか。これで５回目だ。宿題は？

亮介：えっと…忘れてしまいました。すみません。

Ryōsuke: A, yabai! Nebō shichatta.
Densha icchata ka na…

Gakkō ni tsuita ato...

Ryōsuke: Sumimasen, densha ni noriokurete shimaimashita.

Kyōshi: Mata ka. Kore de go-kaime da. Shukudai wa?

Ryōsuke: Etto...wasurete shimaimashita. Sumimasen.

Using ～てしまう

Giving advice or warnings about a potentially regrettable outcome:

そんなに食べたら、おなかが痛くなってしまいますよ。
Sonna ni tabetara, onaka ga itaku natte shimaimasu yo.
If you eat such a huge amount of food, your stomach will hurt.

Expressing regret or sadness about an action or outcome:

好きなドラマが今日で終わってしまいました。
Sukina dorama ga kyou de owatte shimaimashita.
My favorite drama ended today.

Indicating a mistake:

彼の名前を間違えちゃった！
Kare no namae o machigaechatta!
I called him by the wrong name!

Showing that you've made up your mind to do something:

明日は仕事がないから、たくさん飲んじゃおう！
Ashita wa shigoto ga nai kara, takusan nonjaou!
I don't have to work tomorrow, so I'm gonna drink a lot!

Indicating that the verb's action is completed:

もう今日の仕事は全部終わっちゃったよ♪
Mō kyou no shigoto wa zenbu owacchata yo.
I already finished all my work today.

Translation

Ryōsuke: Oh, damn! I overslept.
I wonder if the train has left.

After arriving at school...

Ryōsuke: I'm sorry, I missed the train.

Teacher: Again? This is the fifth time. How about your homework?

Ryōsuke: Um...I forgot it. I'm sorry.

新しい言葉 New Words

- □ヤバイ damn
- □のりおくれる to miss (a train)
- □寝坊しちゃった (ねぼうする) overslept
- □宿題 homework

Lesson 29 I want you to come with me.

[te-form]

私と一緒に **来て** ほしい。

Watashi to issho ni **kite** hoshii.

例 Ex. 見てほしいものがあります。
Mite hoshii mono ga arimasu.

部屋が散らかっているから、片づけてほしい。
Heya ga chikatte iru kara, katazukete hoshii.

それは秘密なので、聞かないでほしい。
Sore wa himitsu nanode, kikanaide hoshii.

> 散らかって（散らかる） *to be messy*
> 片づけて（かたづける） *to tidy up*
> 秘密 *secret*

Point!

- Use ～てほしい when you want someone else to do something. Use ～たい when you want to do something yourself.

  I want to eat → 食べたい　　I want you to eat → 食べてほしい

- To say that you don't want someone to do something, add でほしい to the nai-form of the verb.

  I don't want you to eat → 食べないでほしい

Dialogue Ogawa has a request for her neighbor Mike.

小川：	あの、来週コミュニティセンターでクリスマスのイベントに参加してほしいんですが。	**Ogawa:**	Ano, raishū komyuniti-sentā de kurisumasu no ibento ni sanka shite hoshii n desu ga.
マイク：	はい、いいですよ。たのしそうですね。	**Maiku:**	Hai, ii desu yo. Tanoshi sō desu ne.
小川：	実は、マイクさんにサンタクロースになってほしいんです。	**Ogawa:**	Jitsu wa, Maiku-san ni Santa Kurōsu ni natte hoshii n desu.
マイク：	えっ、私が？	**Maiku:**	E, watashi ga?
小川：	子供たちにプレゼントを渡してメリークリスマスと言って欲しいんです。	**Ogawa:**	Kodomotachi ni purezento o watashite "Merī Kurisumasu" to itte hoshii n desu.

～てしまう with のです(んです)

Since one of the functions of のです and the casual equivalent んです is to indicate a request, you will quite often find them used together with expressions such as ～てほしい and ～たい. Think of んです as marking your request so that the listener can understand your ultimate question, which often goes unstated (see the parenthesized section in the second example below).

今日、家に来てほしいんだけど、いい？
Kyou, uchi ni kite hoshii n dakedo, ii?
I want you to come to my place today, is that OK?

このくつを直してほしいんですが…
(できますか？ いいですか？)
Kono kutsu o naoshite hoshii n desu ga...(dekimasu ka? ii desu ka?)
I want you to fix this shoe...(but can you? will you?)

If you want to be more polite, use ～てもらいたい:

レポートを見てもらいたいんですが。
Repōto o mite moraitai n desu ga.
I'd like you to take a look at my report.

What's the difference? してほしくない vs. しないでほしい

Both of these indicate that you want someone to not do an action; してほしくない is focused more on expressing your opinion, whereas the stronger しないでほしい is used when you really want to prevent the person from doing the activity.

今、家に来てほしくない。
Ima, uchi ni kite hoshikunai.
I don't want you to come home right now.

今、家に来ないでほしい。
Ima, uchi ni konaide hoshii.
I want you to not come home now.

心配してほしくない。
shinpai shite hoshikunai.
don't worry about me

心配しないでほしい。
shinpai shinaide hoshii.
leave me alone

Translation

Ogawa: I want you to join our Christmas event at the community center next week.
Mike: Sure, sounds fun.
Ogawa: Actually, I want you to be Santa Claus.
Mike: Uh, me?
Ogawa: I want you to give the children presents and tell them "Merry Christmas."

新しい言葉 New Words

- □となりの next door
- □参加 participate
- □実は Actually,
- □渡して(わたす) to hand out

Lesson 30 I will invite her and see.

[te-form]

彼女を **誘って** みます。

Kanojo o **sasotte** mimasu.

例 Ex. 食べてみたいです。
Tabete mitai desu.

電話してみましょう。
Denwa shite mimashou.

この服、着てみたけど、きつかったです。
Kono fuku, kite mita kedo, kitsukatta desu.

誘って(さそう) *to invite*
服 *cloth*
きつい *tight*

Point!

- ～てみる is used when trying something for the first time or when you are unsure what will happen.
- みる can be conjugated to express things like *want to try* (～てみたい) and *tried* (～てみた).
- Be careful not to confuse this usage with the standalone みたい, which means *want to see*.

Dialogue Jenna is talking with her Japanese teacher.

先生： 抹茶を飲んだことがありますか？
ジェナ： いえ、ないです。飲んでみたいです。
先生： 今度お茶会があるので、来てみませんか？
ジェナ： はい、ぜひ、行ってみたいです。
先生： 着物もありますから、着てみますか？
ジェナ： はい。お願いします！

Sensei: Maccha o nonda koto ga arimasu ka?
Jena: Ie, nai desu. Nonde mitai desu.
Sensei: Kondo ochakai ga aru node, kite mimasen ka?
Jena: Hai, zehi itte mitai desu.
Sensei: Kimono mo arimasu kara, kite mimasu ka?
Jena: Hai. Onegai shimasu!

Using ～てみる

When talking about doing something for the first time:

北海道に行ってみたい。
Hokkaidō ni itte mitai.
I want to go to Hokkaidō.

オーロラをみてみたい。
Ōrora o mite mitai.
I want to see the aurora.

When you are not sure about the outcome of the action:

先生に聞いてみる。
Sensei ni kiite miru.
I'll ask my teacher and see.

とにかく、やってみる。
Tonikaku, yatte miru.
Anyways, I'll try it and see what happens.

Watch out!

～てみた is used to indicate that you tried something, but it can't be used in situations where you tried and failed (or the outcome was similarly unfavorable). For that you need to use volitional form, which we will examine in an upcoming lesson.

食べてみました。
Tabete mimashita.
I tried (eating) it for the first time.

食べようとしたけど、だめだった。
Tabeyou to shita kedo, dame datta.
I tried (eating) it, but I didn't like it.

Translation

Teacher: Have you ever tried maccha?
Jenna: No, I haven't. I want to try it.
Teacher: We are having a tea party sometime soon, would you like to come?
Jenna: Sure, I'd love to.
Teacher: I have a kimono too, do you want to try it on?
Jenna: Yes, please!

新しい言葉 New Words

- ☐抹茶 powdered green tea
- ☐今度 in the near future
- ☐お茶会 tea ceremony
- ☐ぜひ I'd love to; by all means

Simple Past Tense

たけい / ないけいかこ ta-form / past nai-form

These simple past forms are used in casual conversation.

ta-form conjugates the same as te-form, so the exceptions noted there apply here as well (for example, 行く conjugates to 行った and 行かなかった). The past version of nai-form ends with かった , just like we saw with i-adjectives.

Group 1

	ta-form		past nai-form	
meet	会った	atta	会わなかった	awanakatta
sing	歌った	utatta	歌わなかった	utawanakatta
buy	買った	katta	買わなかった	kawanakatta
say	言った	itta	言わなかった	iwanakatta
differ	違った	chigatta	違わなかった	chigawanakatta
pay	払った	haratta	払わなかった	harawanakatta
use	使った	tsukatta	使わなかった	tsukawanakatta
hold	持った	motta	持たなかった	motanakatta
wait	待った	matta	待たなかった	matanakatta
stand	立った	tatta	立たなかった	tatanakatta
take	取った	totta	取らなかった	toranakatta
enter	入った	haitta	入らなかった	hairanakatta
make	作った	tsukutta	作らなかった	tsukuranakatta
send	送った	okutta	送らなかった	okuranakatta
know	知った	shitta	知らなかった	shiranakatta
ride	乗った	notta	乗らなかった	noranakatta
cut	切った	kitta	切らなかった	kiranakatta
be troubled	困った	komatta	困らなかった	komaranakatta
return	帰った	kaetta	帰らなかった	kaeranakatta
climb	登った	nobotta	登らなかった	noboranakatta
sleep	眠った	nemutta	眠らなかった	nemuranakatta
choose	選んだ	eranda	選ばなかった	erabanakatta
carry	運んだ	hakonda	運ばなかった	hakobanakatta
call	呼んだ	yonda	呼ばなかった	yobanakatta
fall	転んだ	koronda	転ばなかった	korobanakatta
live	住んだ	sunda	住まなかった	sumanakatta
be crowded	混んだ	konda	混まなかった	komanakatta
read	読んだ	yonda	読まなかった	yomanakatta

rest	休んだ	yasunda	休まなかった	yasumanakatta
write	書いた	kaita	書かなかった	kakanakatta
arrive	着いた	tsuita	着かなかった	tsukanakatta
hear/listen/ask	聞いた	kiita	聞かなかった	kikanakatta
walk	歩いた	aruita	歩かなかった	arukanakatta
swim	泳いだ	oyoida	泳がなかった	oyoganakatta
hurry	急いだ	isoida	急がなかった	isoganakatta
hand or pass	渡した	watashita	渡さなかった	watasanakatta
lend or rent	貸した	kashita	貸さなかった	kasanakatta
give back	返した	kaeshita	返さなかった	kaesanakatta
look for	探した	sagashita	探さなかった	sagasanakatta
talk or speak	話した	hanashita	話さなかった	hanasanakatta

Group 2

	ta-form		past nai-form	
wake	起きた	okita	起きなかった	okinakatta
go to bed	寝た	neta	寝なかった	nenakatta
open	開けた	aketa	開けなかった	akenakatta
close	閉めた	shimeta	閉めなかった	simenakatta
put in	入れた	ireta	入れなかった	irenakatta
see/look/watch	見た	mita	見なかった	minakatta
teach	教えた	oshieta	教えなかった	oshienakatta
show	見せた	miseta	見せなかった	misenakatta
stop	止めた	tometa	止めなかった	tomenakatta
forget	忘れた	wasureta	忘れなかった	wasurenakatta
wear	着た	kita	着なかった	kinakatta

Group 3

	ta-form		past nai-form	
do	した	shita	しなかった	shinakatta
come	来た	kita	来なかった	konakatta

Lesson 31 Did you go somewhere yesterday?

[ta-form]

昨日どっか **行った** ？

Kinou dokka **itta** ?

例 Ex. 今朝、7時に起きた。
Kesa, shichi-ji ni okita.

仕事終わったの？
Shigoto owatta no?

先週富士山に登ったよ。
Senshū Fuji-san ni nobotta yo.

どっか（どこか） *somewhere*
今朝 *this morning*
登った（のぼる） *to climb*

Point!

- ta-form follows the same rules as the present tenses you already learned (dictionary form and nai-form).
- It is used to express the simple past tense.

Dialogue A boy is talking to his mother after returning from school.

母： お帰り。学校どうだった？
息子： ふつう。
母： 何したの？
息子： え、ふつうに英語とか数学とか勉強したよ。
母： テストはなかったの？
息子： なかったよ。ああ、そういえばなんかお知らせもらったよ。

Haha: Okaeri. Gakkō dō datta?
Musuko: Futsū.
Haha: Nani shita no?
Musuko: E, futsū ni eigo toka sūgaku toka benkyō shita yo.
Haha: Tesuto wa nakatta no?
Musuko: Nakatta yo. Ā, sō ieba nanka o-shirase moratta yo.

Indefinite pronouns in Japanese

も	なにも *nothing*	どこも *nowhere*	だれも *no one*	どちらも *neither*	どれも *none*

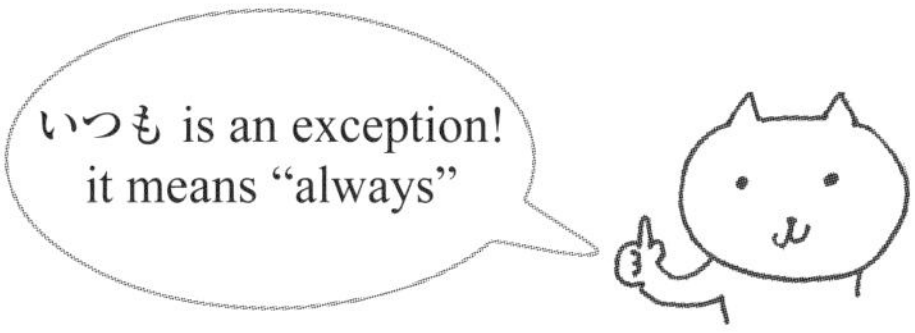

でも	なんでも *anything*	どこでも *anywhere*	だれでも *anyone*	どちらでも *either*	どれでも *any (of them)*	いつでも *anytime*

か	なにか *something*	どこか *somewhere*	だれか *someone*	どちらか *one (of the two)*	どれか *one (of them)*	いつか *someday*

Watch out!

Grammatical particles are attached to the above indefinite pronouns just as they are to other nouns:

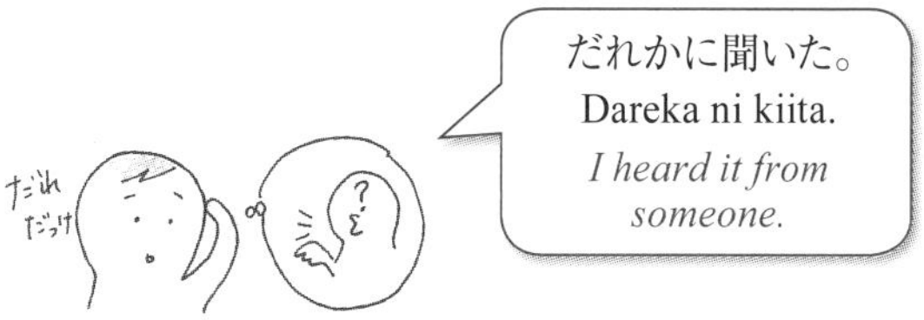

But if the indefinite pronoun ends in も, the grammatical particle is placed before the も:

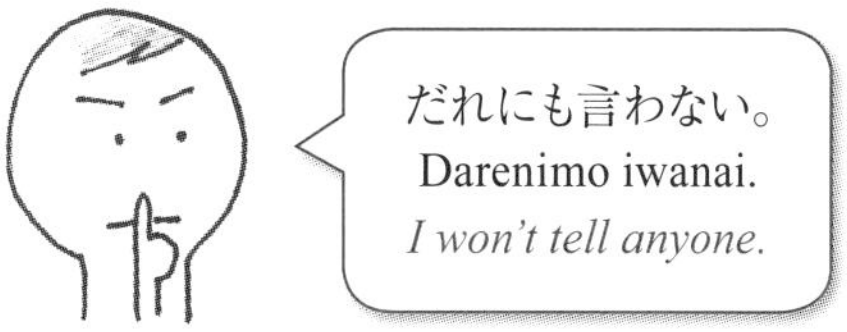

Translation

Mother: Hey, how was school?
Son: It was normal.
Mother: What did you do?
Son: Um, we studied English and math as usual.
Mother: You didn't have a test?
Son: No. Oh that reminds me, I got some letter from school.

新しい言葉 New Words

- □数学 math
- □ふつう normal
- □ふつうに as usual
- □そういえば that reminds me
- □なんか(なにか) something (casual)
- □お知らせ letter; notification

Lesson 32 I did laundry, and went shopping...

た form ＋り＋する　to do one of several activities

[ta-form]		[ta-form]		
洗濯した	り	買い物した	り	しました。
Sentaku shita	ri	kaimono shita	ri	shimasita.

例 Ex. 休みの日は映画を見たり、本を読んだりします。
Yasumi no hi wa eiga o mitari, hon o yondari shimasu.

階段を上ったり下りたりして疲れました。
Kaidan o nobottari oritari shite tsukaremashita.

何か作ったりするのが好きです。
Nanika tsukuttari suru no ga suki desu.

休みの日 *day off*
洗濯 *laundry*
買い物 *shopping*
上ったり下りたり（のぼる・おりる） *to go up and down*
作ったりする（つくる） *to make things (among other activities)*

Point!

- ～たり is used when listing activities. Usually two or more activities are listed, but sometimes only one activity is stated with others being implied.
- The verb that follows ～たり must be some form of する (して, します, したい, etc.).
- This construction can also be used to express that the activities are repeated over and over.

Dialogue Anne wants to join an international exchange club.

アン：この国際交流クラブってなにするんですか？
太田：主に、みんなでしゃべったり、いっしょに料理つくったりしてます。
アン：歌ったり踊ったりもしますか？
太田：いいえ、あんまり…

An: Kono kokusai kōryū kurabu tte nani suru n desu ka?
Ōta: Omo ni, minna de shabettari, issho ni ryōri tsukuttari shitemasu.
An: Utattari odottari mo shimasu ka?
Ōta: Iie, anmari…

What's the difference? 〜たり vs. 〜て

Let's say someone asks you the question:
今日なにをしましたか？ *What did you do today?*

We already learned that the te-form of a verb can be used to list the activities that you did. So how is that different from listing them with 〜たり?

When you connect verbs using te-form, you are implying that they occurred in chronological order—just like when you tell a story. So to answer the above question, for example, you could say:

> 朝起きて、仕事をして、ご飯を食べて、友達と映画を見て、家に帰って、寝ました。
> Asa okite, shigoto o shite, gohan o tabete, tomodachi to eiga o mite, uchi ni kaette, nemashita.
> *I woke up, went to work, ate lunch, saw a movie with a friend, then came home and went to sleep.*

But if you just want to respond with the noteworthy activities you did today, you can use 〜たり:

> 仕事したり、友達と映画を見たりしました。
> Shigoto shitari, tomodachi to eiga o mitari shimashita.
> *I went to work and also saw a movie with a friend.*

Note that 〜たり generally can't be used to list mundane activities that everyone does daily (things like waking up, sleeping, or going to the bathroom).

Repeated activities

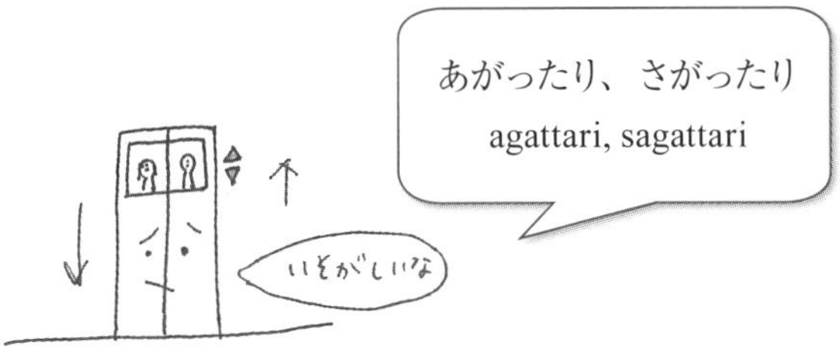

Translation

Anne: What sort of things does this international exchange club do?

Ōta: We mainly chat with each other and cook food, things like that.

Anne: Do you do stuff like dancing and singing, too?

Ōta: No, not really…

新しい言葉 New Words

- ☐国際交流 international exchange
- ☐主に mainly
- ☐しゃべったり（おしゃべりする） to chat
- ☐踊ったり（おどる） to dance
- ☐あんまり not really

Lesson 33 I will call you when I get there.

[ta-form]

そちらに **着いた** ら、電話します。

Sochira ni **tsuita** ra, denwa shimasu.

例 Ex. 日本に行ったら、色んな料理を食べたいです。
Nihon ni ittara, ironna ryōri o tabetai desu.

9時になったら、始めましょうか？
Ku-ji ni nattara, hajimemashou ka?

3月の終わりになったら桜が咲き始めますよ。
San-gatsu no owari ni nattara sakura ga sakihajimemasu yo.

着いたら（つく） *to arrive*
色んな *various*
なったら（なる） *to become*
3月の終わり *the end of March*
咲き始めます *to start blooming*

Point!

- ～たら can translate to *when*, *after*, or *if* in English, depending on the sentence. It implies that what follows will occur once the preceding condition is true.
- You can also use ～たら to talk about things that happened in the past, but doing so implies that what happened next was unexpected:

ドアを開けたら、雪が降っていた！ → When I opened the door, it was snowing!

Dialogue Two coworkers are conversing at the office.

西岡：あ、もう５時ですね。	**Nishioka:** A, mō go-ji desu ne.
マイケル：ええ。この仕事が終わったら帰りたいな。	**Maikeru:** Ē. Kono shigoto ga owattara kaeritai na.
西岡：終わったら飲みに行きませんか？	**Nishioka:** Owattara nomi ni ikimasen ka?
マイケル：すみません、終わったらすぐ家に帰らないといけないので…… ７時になったらオンラインポーカーゲームがはじまりますから。	**Maikeru:** Sumimasen, owattara sugu uchi ni kaeranai to ikenai node… Shichi-ji ni nattara onrain pōkā gēmu ga hajimarimasu kara.
西岡：……	**Nishioka:** ...

What's the difference? ～てから vs. ～たら

As we've already learned, ～てから is used to stress that an action needs to take place before another action. Although the action that precedes ～たら does occur prior to the following action, it doesn't carry this nuance.

宿題がおわってから遊ぶ。 Shukudai ga owatte kara asobu. *Before I play, I need to finish my homework.*	宿題が終わったら遊ぶ。 Shukudai ga owattara asobu. *Once I finish my homework, I'm gonna play.*

One more thing!

～たら is also used for actions that are uncertain or unlikely to occur.

100 万ドルあったら、何をしますか？ Hyakuman doru attara, nani o shimasu ka? *What would you do if you had a million dollars?*	宇宙人に会ったら、いっしょに写真をとります。 Uchūjin ni attara, issho ni shashin o torimasu. *If I met an alien, I would take a picture with it.*

If you want ～たら to mean *if* rather than *when*, you can add もし for clarification since it also means *if* (you still have to say ～たら, though).

結婚したら…
Kekkon shitara..

If I get married?
When I get married?
I don't know which it is...

もし結婚したら、家を買いたいです。
Moshi kekkon shitara, uchi o kaitai desu.
If I get married, I want to buy a house.

Translation

Nishioka: Oh, it's already five o'clock.

Michael: Yeah, I wanna go home after I finish this job.

Nishioka: Want to grab some drinks after we finish?

Michael: Sorry, I have to go home as soon as we're done.
There's an online poker game starting at seven.

Nishioka: ...

新しい言葉 New Words

- ☐ 7時になったら（なる） at seven o'clock
- ☐ オンライン online
- ☐ ポーカーゲーム poker game

Lesson 34 You should clean your room.

＿＿＿＿ ほうがいい　**should ＿＿＿; had better ＿＿＿**

[ta-form]

部屋を掃除 した ほうがいいですよ。

Heya o sōji shita hō ga ii desu yo.

そろそろ　*soon, before long*
急いだ（いそぐ）　*to hurry*
飲み会　*drinking party*
払った（はらう）　*to pay*

例 Ex. 彼女に謝ったほうがいいですよ。
Kanojo ni ayamatta hō ga ii desu yo.

そろそろ始まるので、急いだほうがいいですね。
Sorosoro hajimaru node, isoida hō ga ii desu ne.

飲み会のお金を、今払ったほうがいいですか？
Nomikai no okane o, ima haratta hō ga ii desu ka?

Point!

- Try not to add any pauses between the verb and the ほうがいい that follows it; they should sound like a single word.
- We already learned how to use ほうがいい to tell someone that they shouldn't do something (see page 64).

Dialogue Rob noticed that his friend Mori doesn't look well.

ロブ：森さん、どうしたんですか。元気ないですね。	**Robu:** Mori-san, dō shita n desu ka. Genki nai desu ne.
森：うん。なんだか体がだるくて、やる気が出ないんですよ。	**Mori:** Un. Nandaka karada ga darukute, yaruki ga denai n desu yo.
ロブ：何か食べたほうがいいですよ、お昼たべてないでしょ？	**Robu:** Nanika tabeta hō ga ii desu yo. O-hiru tabetenai desho?
森：食欲もなくて。夜も眠れないし。	**Mori:** Shokuyoku mo nakute. Yoru mo nemurenai shi.
ロブ：病院に行ったほうがいいですよ。	**Robu:** Byōin ni itta hō ga ii desu yo.

Making Suggestions

In addition to ほうがいい, there is another expression you can use when giving advice: ～たらどうですか, which is similar to saying in English, "Why don't you..."

頭が痛いんです。
Atama ga itai n desu.
My head hurts.

→

薬を飲んだほうがいいですよ
Kusuri o nonda hō ga ii desu yo.
You should take some medicine.

薬を飲んだらどうですか?
Kusuri o nondara dō desu ka?
Why don't you take some medicine?

You can also use ～てみる with this expression:

行ってみたらどうですか?
Itte mitara dō desu ka?
Why don't you go and see?

One more thing!

The exact meaning of なんだか depends on the sentence, but it is usually close to the English *somehow*, *somewhat*, *kind of*, or *for some reason*.

なんだかつかれた。
Nandaka tsukareta.
I'm kind of tired.

なんだかよく分からないけど…
Nandaka yoku wakaranai kedo...
I don't know why but for some reason...

What's the difference? 寝る(ねる) vs. 眠る(ねむる)

寝る means *to lay down* or *to go to bed*, while 眠る means *to sleep*.

お父さんはベットで寝ています。
Otōsan wa beddo de nete imasu.
Dad's laying on the bed.

昨日の夜よく眠れました。
Kinou no yoru yoku nemuremashita.
I was able to sleep well last night.

Translation

Rob: What's wrong, Mori? You look down.
Mori: Yeah. For some reason I'm sluggish and I don't feel like doing anything.
Rob: You should eat something. You didn't eat lunch, right?
Mori: No appetite. I also can't sleep at night.
Rob: You'd better go to the clinic.

新しい言葉 New Words

- □なんだか for some reason
- □だるくて(だるい) sluggish
- □やる気 motivation
- □でしょ?(でしょう) right?
- □食欲 appetite
- □眠れない(ねむる) can't sleep

Lesson 35 I just got home.

[ta-form]

今 **帰った** ばかりです。

Ima kaetta bakari desu.

例 Ex. さっき空港に着いたばかりです。
Sakki kūkō ni tsuita bakari desu.

この靴は昨日買ったばかりなので、まだ履いていません。
Kono kutsu wa kinou katta bakari nanode mada haite imasen.

そのケーキは焼いたばっかりだから、熱いよ。
Sono kēki wa yaita bakkari dakara, atsui yo.

空港 *airport*
まだ履いていません *haven't yet worn*
ケーキ *cake*
焼いた(やく) *to bake*
さっき *just a minute ago*

Point!

- ～たばかり is used to show that the action of a verb has just finished.
- In informal situations, ばかり often becomes ばっかり or ばっか.

Dialogue A couple is talking on the phone after work.

彼女：もしもし？ 仕事おわった？
彼氏：いま、終わったばかりだよ。
彼女：近くのイタリアンレストラン行かない？先週できたばかりの。
彼氏：でも昨日イタリアン食べたばっかじゃん。
彼女：だめ？ 今予約したばかりだよ……
彼氏：もう予約しちゃったの？ しょうがないな。

Kanojo: Moshimoshi? Shigoto owatta?
Kareshi: Ima, owatta bakari da yo.
Kanojo: Chikaku no Itarian resutoran ikanai? Senshū dekita bakari no.
Kareshi: Demo kinou Itarian tabeta bakka jan.
Kanojo: Dame? Ima yoyaku shita bakkari da yo...
Kareshi: Mō yoyaku shichatta no? Shōganai na.

What's the difference? ばかり vs. ところ

These two expressions are very similar; the main difference is that ところ is focused on the point in time that the action finished, whereas ばかり places more emphasis on the action itself. That's why ばかり can also be used to indicate that something freshly or newly occurred. Sometimes the two are interchangeable...

駅に着いたばかりです。
Eki ni tsuita bakari desu.
I just arrived at the train station.

=

駅に着いたところです。
Eki ni tsuita tokoro desu.
I just arrived at the station.

These are the same.

...and sometimes they are not:

会社に入ったばかりです。
Kaisha ni haitta bakari desu.
I just started working at the company.

会社に入ったところです。
Kaisha ni haitta tokoro desu.
Kaisha ni haitta tokoro desu.

These are different.

Watch out!

When the て form of a verb comes before ばかり, it has a different meaning: *all the time.*

うちの子供と夫はゲームしてばかり。
Uchi no kodomo to otto wa gēmu shite bakari.
My husband and kid are constantly playing video games.

仕事してばかりで、つまらない。
Shigoto shite bakari de tsumaranai.
Doing nothing but work is boring.

Also, you can't use ばかり to mean *just* in the following situations:

一つだけ
hitotsu dake
just one

コーヒーだけ
kōhī dake
just coffee

Translation

Girl: Hey, are you off work?

Boy: I just finished.

Girl: Wanna go the Italian restaurant nearby? The one that just opened last week.

Boy: But we just ate Italian yesterday, you know.

Girl: You don't want to? I just made a reservation.

Boy: You already made a reservation? I guess we don't have a choice, then.

新しい言葉 New Words

- □じゃん you know (very casual)
- □しょうがない there's no choice

Chapter 2

Lesson 36 I fell asleep with the TV on.

[ta-form]

テレビを　つけた　まま、寝てしまいました。

Terebi o　tsuketa　mama,　nete shimaimashita.

つけた（つける）	*to turn on*
出かけた（でかける）	*to head out*
妹	*younger sister*
汚れた（よごれる）	*to get dirty*
過ごします（すごす）	*to pass time*

例 Ex. 窓を開けたまま、出かけました。
Mado o aketa mama, dekakemashita.

妹は手が汚れたままで料理を作った。
Imōto wa te ga yogoreta mama de ryōri o tsukutta.

今日は休みだから、パジャマを着たままで過ごします。
Kyou wa yasumi dakara, pajama o kita mama de sugoshimasu.

Point!

- ～たまま is used when the action or state described by the verb remains unchanged.
- Since まま is a noun, it is connected to the word that follows it using the same particle you would use for any other noun in that situation (although the particle is often omitted).

Dialogue Joan is visiting the home of his Japanese friend.

野村：　いらっしゃい。
ジョーン：お邪魔します。わあ、素敵な家ですね。
野村：　いえいえ、散らかったままで…… こちらにどうぞ。
ジョーン：これは畳ですね？
野村：　ええ、和室です。スリッパを履いたまま入れませんよ。
ジョーン：あ、すみません。

Nomura: Irasshai.
Jōn: O-jama shimasu. Wā, suteki na ie desu ne.
Nomura: Ieie, chirakatta mama de…kochira ni dōzo.
Jōn: Kore wa tatami desu ne?
Nomura: Ē, washitsu desu. Surippa o haita mama hairemasen yo.
Jōn: A, sumimasen.

What's the difference? まま vs. ぱなし

ぱなし is a related expression that means the same thing as まま, but it is less formal and can only be used with the masu-stem of verbs.

電気つけっぱなしだよ。 Denki tsukeppanashi da yo. *You left the light on.*	電気をつけたままですよ。 Denki tsuketa mama desu yo. *You left the light on.*

Watch out!

Because まま indicates a current state, it can't be used with the negative past form (～なかった) of a verb—use the present negative form instead and let the form of the verb at the end of the sentence indicate when the statement took place.

歯みがきしなかった
hamigaki shinakatta
didn't brush my teeth

→

寝た
neta
went to sleep

→

歯みがきしないまま寝た
hamigaki shinai mama neta
went to sleep without brushing my teeth

気持ちを言えなかった
kimochi o ienakatta
couldn't tell my feelings

→

別れた
wakareta
broke up

→

気持ちを言えないまま別れた
kimochi o ienai mama wakareta
broke up without telling my feelings

One more thing

まま can be used with nouns and adjectives, too.

生のまま
nama no mama
without cooking

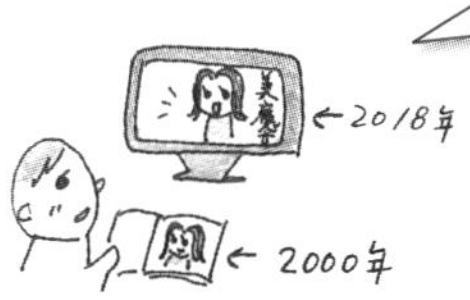

きれいなまま
kirei na mama
still beautiful

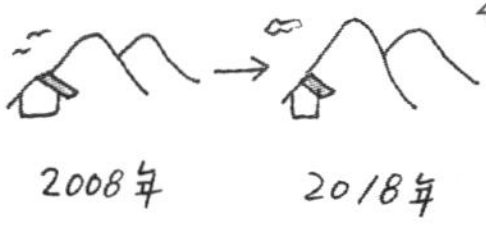

10年前のまま
jūnen mae no mama
the as same as ten years ago

And here is a useful set phrase:

そのままでいいです。
Sono mama de ii desu.
Just like that is fine.

Translation

Nomura: Welcome.

Joan: Thank you for inviting me. Wow, you have a nice house!

Nomura: Oh no, sorry it's all messy…come on in.

Joan: This is tatami, right?

Nomura: Yes, this is a Japanese-style room. You can't enter it with your slippers on.

Joan: Oh, sorry.

新しい言葉 New Words

- ☐畳 tatami mat
- ☐和室 Japanese-style room
- ☐スリッパ slippers

いこうけい Volitional form

When used to make a suggestion, the volitional form is equivalent to *let's <verb>* in English. It is less formal than 〜ましょう .

The casual volitional form can also be used to express one's intentions. Note that in all cases, the final う is not pronounced—use a long お sound (ō) instead.

To conjugate a dictionary-form verb into volitional form:

Group 1 —change the final う to おう

Group 2 —change the final る to よう

Some intransitive verbs don't have a volitional form because it doesn't make sense to use them for suggestions or expressing intentions (違う , 混む , etc.).

Group 1

	dictionary form		volitional form	
to meet	会う	au	会おう	aou
to sing	歌う	utau	歌おう	utaou
to buy	買う	kau	買おう	kaou
to say	言う	iu	言おう	iou
to differ	違う	chigau		
to pay	払う	harau	払おう	haraou
to use	使う	tsukau	使おう	tsukaou
to hold	持つ	motsu	持とう	motou
to wait	待つ	matsu	待とう	matou
to stand	立つ	tatsu	立とう	tatou
to take	取る	toru	取ろう	torou
to enter	入る	hairu	入ろう	hairou
to make	作る	tsukuru	作ろう	tsukurou
to send	送る	okuru	送ろう	okurou
to know	知る	shiru	知ろう	shirou
to ride	乗る	noru	乗ろう	norou
to cut	切る	kiru	切ろう	kirou
to be troubled	困る	komaru		
to return	帰る	kaeru	帰ろう	kaerou
to climb	登る	noboru	登ろう	noborou
to sleep	眠る	nemuru	眠ろう	nemurou
to choose	選ぶ	erabu	選ぼう	erabou
to carry	運ぶ	hakobu	運ぼう	hakobou
to call	呼ぶ	yobu	呼ぼう	yobou
to fall	転ぶ	korobu	転ぼう	korobou
to live	住む	sumu	住もう	sumou
to be crowded	混む	komu		
to read	読む	yomu	読もう	yomou

to rest	休む	yasumu	休もう	yasumou
to write	書く	kaku	書こう	kakou
to arrive	着く	tsuku	着こう	tsukou
to hear/listen/ask	聞く	kiku	聞こう	kikou
to walk	歩く	aruku	歩こう	arukou
to swim	泳ぐ	oyogu	泳ごう	oyogou
to hurry	急ぐ	isogu	急ごう	isogou
to hand or pass	渡す	watasu	渡そう	watasou
to lend or rent	貸す	kasu	貸そう	kasou
to give back	返す	kaesu	返そう	kaesou
to look for	探す	sagasu	探そう	sagasou
to talk or speak	話す	hanasu	話そう	hanasou

Group 2

	dictionary form		volitional form	
to wake	起きる	okiru	起きよう	okiyou
to sleep	寝る	neru	寝よう	neyou
to open	開ける	akeru	開けよう	akeyou
to close	閉める	shimeru	閉めよう	shimeyou
to put in	入れる	ireru	入れよう	ireyou
to see/look/watch	見る	miru	見よう	miyou
to teach	教える	oshieru	教えよう	oshieyou
to show	見せる	miseru	見せよう	miseyou
to stop	止める	tomeru	止めよう	tomeyou
to forget	忘れる	wasureru	忘れよう	wasureyou
to wear	着る	kiru	着よう	kiyou

Group 3

	dictionary form		volitional form	
to do	する	suru	しよう	shiyou
to come	来る	kuru	来よう	koyou

Lesson 37 Let's take a walk.

[volitional form]

散歩に **行こう。**

Sanpo ni **ikou.**

例 Ex. いっしょにジョギングしよう。
Issho ni jogingu shiyou.

今晩ラーメンたべようか。
Konban rāmen tabeyou ka.

今日はやめよう。
Kyou wa yameyou.

ジョギング *jogging*
今晩 *tonight*
食べよう *let's eat*
やめよう（やめる） *let's not (do that)*

Point!

- This is the casual version of the volitional form ～ましょう that we learned in *Practical Japanese 1*.
- When followed by か (with or without a question mark), it indicates a suggestion.
- To suggest not to do an action, use やめよう.

Dialogue A husband and wife are discussing their computer.

夫：	このパソコン古くなったし、もう買い替えようかな。	**Otto:**	Kono pasokon furuku natta shi, mō kaikaeyou ka na.
妻：	ねえ、今度の土曜日、秋葉原にパソコン見に行こうよ。	**Tsuma:**	Nē, kondo no doyōbi, Akihabara ni pasokon mi ni ikou yo.
夫：	え～わざわざ秋葉原まで行くの？めんどくさいな。 まずはネットで見てみよう。	**Otto:**	Ē—wazawaza Akihabara made iku no? Mendokusai na. Mazu wa netto de mite miyou.
妻：	ん。わかった。ちょっとその前にコーヒいれようか。	**Tsuma:**	Un, wakatta. Chotto sono mae ni kōhī ireyou ka.

Using casual volitional form

いこう！ Ikou! *Let's go!*	いこうよ Ikou yo *Come on, let's go*	いこうか Ikou ka *Wanna go?*	いこうかな Ikou ka na *I'm thinking about going*

What's the difference? めんどくさい vs. うっとうしい

Both of these words mean *annoying*, but there is a difference between them. めんどくさい is usually used for tasks or jobs (things you do), while うっとうしい is used to describe people, animals, or sounds (things you experience or interact with).

宿題はめんどくさい。 Shukudai wa mendokusai. *(Doing) homework is annoying.*	蚊はうっとうしい。 Ka wa uttōshii. *Mosquitoes are annoying.*

色々な気持ち Various Feelings

疲れた tsukareta *tired*	やる気がない yaruki ga nai *unmotivated*	心配する shinpai suru *worried*	いらいらする iraira suru *irritated*

幸せ shiawase *happy (in life)*	やる気がある yaruki ga aru *motivated*	わくわくする wakuwaku suru *excited*	ほっとする hotto suru *relieved*

Translation

Husband: This computer is old...I'm thinking about buying a new one.

Wife: Hey, let's go to Akihabara this Saturday to checkout some computers.

Husband: Huh—going to all the way to Akihabara? That's annoying. First let's look online.

Wife: Okay. Before we do that, how about I brew some coffee?

新しい言葉 New Words

- □買い替えよう (かいかえる) to buy new
- □わざわざ...まで行く to go all the way to
- □めんどくさい annoying
- □まずは first(ly)
- □いれようか (いれる) to brew (coffee, tea, etc.)

Lesson 38 I'm thinking I will go.

[volitional form]

行こう と思っています。

Ikou to omotte imasu.

例 Ex. いつか世界一周しようと思っています。
Itsuka sekai isshū shiyou to omotte imasu.

彼はネットビジネスをはじめようと思っています。
Kare wa netto bijinesu o hajimeyou to omotte imasu.

これから毎日運動しようと思います。
Korekara mainichi undō shiyou to omoimasu.

世界一周	*trip around the world*
ネットビジネス	*online business*
これから	*from now on*
運動	*physical exercise*

Point!

- ～ようと思う is used to indicate one's intentions, but it doesn't carry the same certainty as つもりです. (see page 115)
- If you've just made the decision, use 思います instead of 思っています (just as you would say "I think I'll..." instead of "I'm thinking that I'll..." in English).

Dialogue A teacher is asking her students about their New Year's resolutions.

先生： 皆さん、今年の抱負は何ですか？
生徒A：私は、漢字を300字覚えようと思います。
生徒B：僕は、早く起きてジョギングしようと思います。先生は？
先生： そうですね…私は去年からやせようとしてますが、いつもダイエットに失敗してしまうので、今年こそは、がんばろうと思ってます。

Sensei: Minasan, kotoshi no hōfu wa nan desu ka?
Seito A: Watashi wa, kanji o 300-ji oboeyou to omoimasu.
Seito B: Boku wa, hayaku okite jogingu shiyou to omoimasu. Sensei wa?
Sensei: Sō desu ne...watashi wa kyonen kara yaseyou to shitemasu ga, itsumo daietto ni shippai shite shimau node, kotoshi koso wa, ganbarou to omottemasu.

What's the difference?　しようと思う vs. すると思う

しようと思う expresses the speaker's intentions, whereas すると思う indicates the speaker's guess. That's why the former can't be used to talk about a third party but the latter can.

日本に行こうと思います！
Nihon ni ikou to omoimasu!
I think I'll go to Japan!

日本に行くと思います。
Nihon ni iku to omoimasu.
I think I might go to Japan.

私は、彼は日本に行くと思います。
Watashi wa, kare wa nihon ni iku to omoimasu.
I think he's going to Japan.

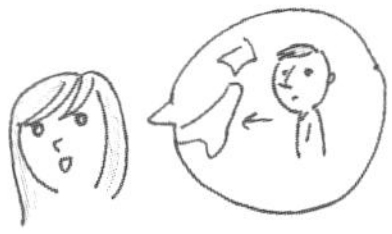

One more thing

～ようと思う　is often used with ～てみる:

うまくいくかどうかわからないけど、やってみようと思います。
Umaku iku ka dō ka wakaranai kedo, yatte miyou to omoimasu.
I don't know whether it will work or not, but I think I'll give it a try.

Using　こそ

こそ places emphasis on the word that precedes it.

何回も試験に落ちたけど、今度こそ合格する！
Nankai mo shiken ni ochita kedo, kondo koso gōkaku suru!
I've failed the exam many times, but I'll pass this time for sure!

青木：　歌が上手ですね。
Aoki：　Uta ga jōzu desu ne.
You're good at singing.

田中：　青木さんこそ上手ですよ。
Tanaka：　Aoki-san koso jōzu desu yo.
You are the one who is good at singing.

こちらこそ is a set phrase you can use when you want to say *I'm the one who should say thank you*.

昨日はありがとうございました。
Kinou wa arigatō gozaimashita.
Thank you for yesterday.

こちらこそ（ありがとうございました）。
Kochira koso (arigatō gozaimashita).
I'm the one who should be thanking you.

Translation

Teacher: So everyone, what are your New Year's resolutions?

Student A: I'm thinking I will memorize 300 kanji.

Student B: I think I will wake up early to go jogging. What about you?

Teacher: Well...I've been trying to lose weight since last year, but I've never stuck to a diet, so this year I'm definitely thinking about working hard on that.

新しい言葉 New Words

- ☐皆さん　everyone
- ☐抱負　resolution
- ☐ジョギング　jogging
- ☐失敗　fail

Lesson 39 I tried to wake up early, but I couldn't.

[volitional form]

早く **起きよう** としたけど、起きられなかった。

Hayaku **okiyou** to shita kedo, okirarenakatta.

例 Ex. さっきの電車に乗ろうとしたけど、乗れませんでした。
Sakki no densha ni norou to shita kedo, noremasen deshita.

(あなたに)連絡しようとしたんですが、連絡先がわかりませんでした。
(Anata ni) renraku shiyou to shita n desu ga, renrakusaki ga wakarimasen deshita.

隣の子が私のテストを見ようとしています。
Tonari no ko ga watashi no tesuto o miyou to shite imasu.

乗ろう(乗る)	*to ride*
連絡	*contact*
連絡先	*contact information*
隣の子	*the kid next to (me)*

Point!

- Use this expression when you want to indicate that you tried or are trying to do something but can't for some reason.
- Don't pause before と when pronouncing this expression.
- The tense must be past (〜ようとした) or present (〜ようとしている) because there is no way to have already failed an action that takes place in the future.

Dialogue Aoki and Mika are discussing their upcoming vacation.

青木：北海道旅行、キャンセルしていい？その日、仕事に行かないといけないから。	**Aoki:** Hokkaidō ryokō, kyanseru shite ii ? Sono hi, shigoto ni ikanai to ikenai kara.
ミカ：仕事？どうして早く言わなかったの？	**Mika:** Shigoto? Dōshite hayaku iwanakatta no?
青木：言おうとしたんだけど、ミカが楽しみにしてたから言えなかったんだ。	**Aoki:** Iou to shita n dakedo, Mika ga tanoshimi ni shiteta kara ienakatta n da.
ミカ：そうだよ。楽しみにしてたのに！どうして断らなかったの？	**Mika:** Sō da yo. Tanoshimi ni shiteta no ni! Dōshite kotowaranakatta no?
青木：断ろうとしたけど、今回の仕事はすごく大切なんだよ。	**Aoki:** Kotowarou to shita kedo, konkai no shigoto wa sugoku taisetsu nan da yo.
ミカ：わたしより仕事が大切？	**Mika:** Watashi yori shigoto ga taisetsu?

The form of する that ends this expression is important

彼はいつも邪魔しようとする。 Kare wa itsumo jama shiyou to suru. *He always tries to bother me.*	彼は邪魔しようとしている。 Kare wa jama shiyou to shite iru. *He's trying to bother me.*	彼は邪魔しようとした。 Kare wa jama shiyou to shita. *He tried to bother me.*

What's the difference? しようとしている vs. するようにしている

~ようにしている is a similar yet unrelated expression. Notice that it uses the particle に instead of と and that the dictionary form of the verb comes before よう. It is used to indicate that you are in the continual process of attempting the action.

毎朝果物を食べるようにしています。 Maiasa kudamono o taberu yō ni shite imasu. *I'm trying to eat fruit every day.*	犬が果物を食べようとしているよ！ Inu ga kudamono o tabeyou to shite iru yo! *The dog is trying to eat the fruit!*

Using のに

のに means *although* or *even though*. It expresses anger, regret, or sadness about an outcome.

彼は嘘をつかないって言ったのに、嘘をついた。
Kare wa uso o tsukanai tte itta noni, uso o tsuita.
Although he said he wouldn't lie to me, he did.

私たちは毎日いっしょうけんめい働いてるのに、お金がたまらない。
Watashi-tachi wa mainichi isshōkenmei hataraite iru noni, okane ga tamaranai.
Even though we work hard everyday, we can't save up any money.

のに can also be used to express your surprise about something that someone else did:

彼は足が痛いのに、最後まで走り続けた。
Kare wa ashi ga itai noni, saigo made hashiritsuzuketa.
Even though his leg was hurting, he kept running all the way to the end.

The part following のに is often omitted if it is obvious from the context:

楽しみにしてたのに！（旅行に行けない）
Tanoshimi ni shiteta noni! (ryokō ni ikenai)
Even though I was looking forward to it! (we can't go on the trip)

Translation

Aoki: Is it okay if we cancel our Hokkaido trip? I have to work that day.

Mika: Work? Why you didn't tell me sooner?

Aoki: I was going to tell you, but you were so looking forward to it that I couldn't.

Mika: Yes, I was really looking forward to it! Why you didn't refuse to go in that day?

Aoki: I tried, but the job this time is very important.

Mika: Your work is more important than me?

新しい言葉 New Words

□断らなかった（ことわる） to refuse
□大切 important

Chapter 3

Plain Style

第3章　普通体

ふつうたい　Plain style

So far, we have learned a number of different forms that verbs can take. With the exception of masu-form, they all belong to the general category of ふつうたい or "plain style."

For the plain style, we use る instead of ます to conjugate te-form and potential form.

じしょけい	食べる	taberu
ないけい	食べない	tabenai
てけい	食べている	tabeteiru
たけい	食べた	tabeta
かのうけい	食べられる	taberareru
いこうけい	食べよう	tabeyou

Contrary to what you might expect from its name, plain style is not limited to informal conversation—it is the main form that verbs take in news articles, reports, and novels.

Plain style is also used for various grammatical patterns. Some of these we've already looked at (～たばかり , for example). This chapter introduces some new ways of using ふつうたい .

Lesson 40 When

～時《toki》（とき）

verb or i-adjective + 時　　na-adjective + な時　　noun + の時

Point!

- This 時 is not used for asking *when* something happens.
- In English, the tense of the verb in a *when* clause indicates when that action occurred in relation to the present time. For example, if you start a sentence with "When I go to Japan...", we know that you are talking about the future because you said *go*, not *went*.
- But in Japanese, the tense of the verb that comes before 時 tells you when that action occurred in relation to the action of the verb at the end of the sentence. That's why you will often encounter ta-form before 時, even though the entire sentence is about actions that will take place in the future.

例 Ex.

家を出るとき、鍵を閉めませんでした。
Uchi o deru toki, kagi o shimemasen deshita.
When I left home, I didn't lock the door.

勉強している時は話しかけないで。
Benkyō shite iru toki wa hanashi kakenaide.
When I am studying, don't talk to me.

いそがしい時は電話をとれません。
Isogashii toki wa denwa o toremasen.
I can't answer the phone when I am busy.

エアコンを使わない時は、コンセントを抜いてください。
Eakon o tsukawanai toki wa, konsento o nuite kudasai.
Please unplug the air conditioner when you aren't using it.

ヒマな時に会いましょう。
Hima na toki ni aimashou.
Let's get together when we are free.

大学生の時、イタリアに留学しました。
Daigakusei no toki, Itaria ni ryūgaku shimashita.
When I was a college student, I studied in Italy.

留学してた時、友達ができましたか？
Ryūgaku shiteta toki, tomodachi ga dekimashita ka?
Did you make any friends while you were studying there?

ええ、だから日本に帰る時は本当に悲しかったです。
Ē, dakara nihon ni kaeru toki wa hontō ni kanashikatta desu.
Yes, so I was really sad when I left for Japan.

帰る時 = *when you leave*

帰った時 = *when you arrive*

Lesson 41 I think

～と《to》思《omo》い《i》ま《ma》す《su》

verb or i-adjective + と思います　noun or na-adjective + だと思います

Point!

- To form the negative, use ～ないと思います (*I think it is not...*).
- For volitional form usage, see page 104.
- と思う and だと思う are the informal variants.

例 Ex.

明日は雪が降ると思います。
Ashita wa yuki ga furu to omoimasu.
I think it will snow tomorrow.

先生は来ないと思います。
Sensei wa konai to omoimasu.
I don't think the teacher will come.

来週は忙しいと思います。
Raishū wa isogashii to omoimasu.
I think I will be busy next week.

再来週はヒマだと思います。
Saraishū wa hima dato omoimasu.
I think I will be free the week after next.

そう思います。
Sō omoimasu.
I think so.

日本のアニメについてどう思いますか
Nihon no anime ni tsuite dō omoimasu ka?
What do you think about Japanese anime?

ちょっと変だと思います。
Chotto hen dato omoimasu.
I think it's a little weird.

僕は変じゃないと思います。
Boku wa hen janai to omoimasu.
I don't think it's weird.

ねえ、このドレスどう思う？
Nē, kono doresu dō omou?
Hey, what do you think about this dress?

いいと思うよ！
Ii to omou yo!
I think it's nice!

Lesson 42 <someone> said

〜と《to》(って《tte》)言《i》って《tte》ま《ma》し《shi》た《ta》。

verb or i-adjective + と (って) 言ってました
noun or na-adjective + だと (って) 言ってました

Point!

- When referencing something that someone else said, Japanese natives typically use 言っていました (or the informal 言っていた) instead of the simple past form of 言った. This is similar to how English natives might say, "So and so was saying that..."
- In conversation, the particle と in this expression becomes って and だと becomes だって. This is just a colloquial contraction that sounds more natural.
- って言ってた and だって言ってた are the casual forms, but sometimes even the 言ってた is omitted and people just say って or だって.
- In addition to plain style, you can also use volitional form with this expression.

例 Ex.

明日は雨が降るって言ってましたよ。
Ashita wa ame ga furu tte ittemashita yo. *They said it will rain tomorrow.*

トムさんが「一緒に映画を見よう」って言ってました。
Tomu-san ga "issho ni eiga o miyou" tte ittemashita. *Tom said, "Let's watch a movie together."*

ジョンさんは日本のテレビは好きじゃないって言ってました。
Jon-san wa nihon no terebi wa suki janai tte ittemashita.
John said he doesn't like Japanese TV shows.

ケビンがみきのこと、かわいいって。
Kebin ga Miki no koto, kawaii tte.
Kevin said Miki is cute.

本当？ でもケビンは由香のこと好きだって言ってたよ。
Hontō? Demo, Kebin wa Yuka no koto suki datte itteta yo.
Really? But he told me he likes you (Yuka).

Lesson 43 intend to

～つもりです《tsu mo ri de su》

verb or i-adjective + つもり　　noun + つもり
na-adjective + なつもり

Point!

- This is used to express your own intentions or beliefs, so it sounds rude if you use it for asking questions or talking about others.
- If you want to ask someone else about their intentions or plans, use 予定ですか (yotei desu ka) instead:

週末は何をする予定ですか？	or	週末の予定は？
Shūmatsu wa nani o suru yotei desu ka?		Shūmatsu no yotei wa?
What are you going to do this weekend?		*What are your plans for this weekend?*

- In terms of the negative, つもりはない is stronger than ないつもり.

あの人に会うつもりはない！	会わないつもりだけど…（わからない）
Ano hito ni au tsumori wa nai!	Awanai tsumori dakedo …（wakaranai）
I have no intention of meeting him!	*I don't plan on meeting him but...(I'm not sure)*

- When used with the ～ている form of a verb, つもり indicates that the speaker thought the action of the verb was taking place, but the situation appears contrary to that.

例 Ex.

いつか日本に住むつもりです。
Itsuka Nihon ni sumu tsumori desu. *I intend to live in Japan someday.*

ガスを止めたつもりでした。
Gasu o tometa tsumori deshita. *I had intended to turn off the gas.*

仕事をがんばってるつもりだけど、うまくいかない。
Shigoto o ganbatteru tsumori dakedo, umaku ikanai.
I thought I was working hard, but this isn't turning out so well.

いつまでも若いつもりでむりしちゃだめだよ。
Itsumademo wakai tsumori de, muri shicha dame da yo.
Don't overdo it thinking you are still young.

若いつもりじゃない、まだ若い！
Wakai tsumori janai, mada wakai!
I don't just think it, I am still young!

バカにしたつもりはないよ。
Baka ni shita tsumori wa nai yo.
I didn't intend to make fun of you.

Lesson 44 might

ka mo shi re ma sen

かもしれません

verb, noun, or adjective + かもしれません

Point!

- The informal version is かもしれない.
- Students sometimes mistake this expression for a negative, since it ends in ません or ない, but it just means *might be* or *may be*. To say *might not be*, put the negative form of a verb or adjective in front of this expression:

  しないかもしれません　早くないかもしれません　店じゃないかもしれません

- しれません and しれない are commonly omitted in casual conversation.

例 Ex.

週末は雪が降るかもしれませんね。
Shūmatsu wa yuki ga furu kamoshiremasen ne. *It might snow this weekend.*

母は今ごろ寝てるかもしれません。
Haha wa imagoro neteru kamoshiremasen. *Mother might be sleeping right now.*

仕事があるから、遊びに行けないかも。
Shigoto ga aru kara, asobi ni ikenai kamo. *I might not be able to hang out since I gotta work.*

家に財布を忘れたかもしれません。
Uchi ni saifu o wasureta kamoshiremasen. *I might have left my wallet at home.*

あの人は中国人かもしれない。
Ano hito wa chūgokujin kamoshirenai. *He may be Chinese.*

これは無料じゃないかも。
Kore wa muryō janai kamo. *This might not be free.*

今セールやってるかもしれない。行ってみる？
Ima sēru yatteru kamoshirenai. Itte miru?
They may be having a sale now. Wanna go see?

まだそんなに安くないかも。少し待とうよ。
Mada sonna ni yasukunai kamo. Sukoshi matou yo.
Might not be so cheap yet. Let's wait a bit.

ん～でもなくなるかも！
N—demo naku naru kamo!
Mmm, but they might be sold out!

Lesson 45 looks like; seems; like

み《mi》た《ta》い《i》で《de》す《su》

verb or i-adjective + みたいです　　noun + みたいです
みたいな + noun　　みたいに + verb

Point!

- みたい means *looks like* or *seems* and is generally based on something the speaker personally witnessed.
- Be careful not to confuse it with <*noun*> がみたいです, which means *want to see* <*noun*>.
- It is often used in conjunction with まるで (*as if*).

例 Ex.

おじいちゃんは散歩に行くみたいです。
Ojīchan wa sanpo ni iku mitai desu. *Looks like Grandpa is going to take a walk.*

青木さん、会社を辞めたみたいですよ。
Aoki-san, kaisha o yameta mitai desu yo. *It seems that Mr. Aoki quit working here.*

赤ちゃんが寝ているみたいだから、静かにしたほうがいい。
Akachan ga nete iru mitai dakara, shizuka ni shita hō ga ii.
It seems the baby is sleeping, so we should be quiet.

彼女はネコみたいですね。
Kanojo wa neko mitai desu ne. *She looks like a cat.*

ネコみたいな彼女がほしい。
Neko mitai na kanojo ga hoshii. *I want a girlfriend that acts like a cat.*

あの子はまるで犬みたいに食べる。
Anoko wa marude inu mitai ni taberu. *That boy eats as if he's a dog.*

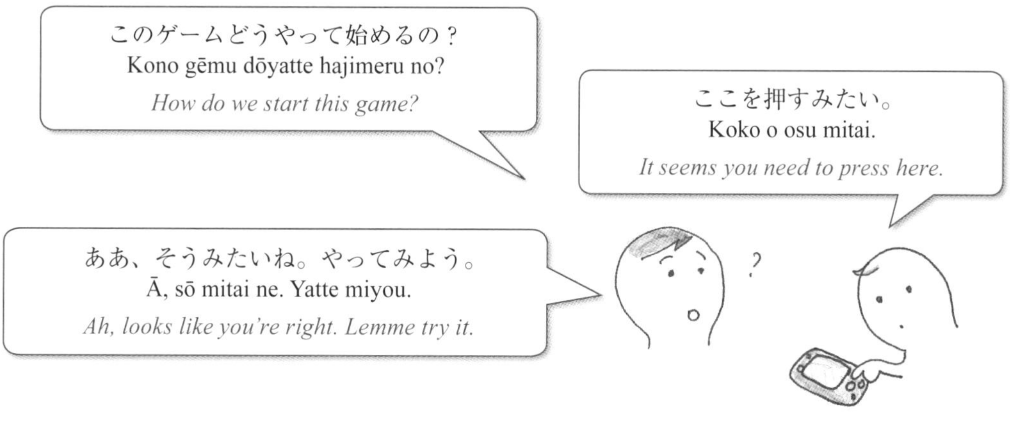

Lesson 46 heard that; it seems

そう《sō》で《de》す《su》

verb or i-adjective + そうです　　noun or na-adjective + そうです

Point!

- そうです is used to indicate something the speaker heard or was told. If the source of the information is not specified, it has a meaning close to *They say that...* or *I heard that...*
- Be especially cautious not to confuse this expression with the one we learned in Lesson 7 on page 28:

楽しいそうです。Tanoshii sō desu.
I heard it's fun.

楽しそうです。Tanoshisō desu.
It seems fun.

雨が降るそうです。Ame ga furu sō desu.
They say it's going to rain.

雨が降りそうです。Ame ga furisō desu.
It looks like it will rain.

例 Ex.

木村さんは結婚したそうです。
Kimura-san wa kekkon o shita sō desu. *I heard Mr. Kimura got married.*

部長は今日は会議に来ないそうです。
Buchō wa kyou wa kaigi ni konai sō desu. *The manager told me he won't be at the meeting today.*

この絵は有名な画家が描いたそうです。
Kono e wa yūmei na gaka ga kaita sō desu. *It says a famous painter drew this picture.*

新幹線のほうが飛行機より便利だそうです。
Shinkansen no hō ga hikōki yori benri da sō desu.
They say the Shinkansen is more convenient than flying.

この家は伝統的な建築だそうです。
Kono ie wa dentōteki na kenchiku da sō desu.
I heard this house was built in a traditional architectural style.

東北はとても寒いそうですから、
コートを持っていったほうがいいですよ。
Tōhoku wa totemo samui sō desu kara, kōto o motte itta hō ga ii desu yo.
I hear the Tōhoku region is very cold, so you should bring a coat with you.

そうですか？
Sō desu ka?
Really?

ええ、もう雪が降り始めたそうですよ。
天気予報で言ってました。
Ē, mō yuki ga furihajimeta sō desu yo. Tenki yohō de ittemashita.
Yes, it seems that the snow has already started falling. They said it on the weather forecast.

Lesson 47 Explanatory *no*

～の《no》で《de》す《su》

verb or i-adjective + のです　　noun or na-adjective + なのです

Point!

- のです can imply a variety of things depending on the situation. Most often, it is used to indicate an explanation (either given or asked for), confirmation, or emphasis.
- Conversationally, this expression is almost always contracted to んです (after verbs and i-adjectives) or なんです (after nouns and na-adjectives).

例 Ex.

すみません、返品したいのですが。
Sumimasen, henpin shitai no desu ga. *Excuse me, I want to return this item.*

大きな荷物ですね。どこに行くんですか。
Ōkina nimotsu desu ne. Doko ni iku n desu ka. *That's a big suitcase. Where are you going?*

静かにして！ 今勉強してるんだ。
Shizuka ni shite! Ima benkyō shiteru n da. *Be quiet! I'm studying now.*

ミカから聞いたんだけど、彼女と別れたの？
Mika kara kiita n dakedo, kanojo to wakareta no?
Did you break up with your girlfriend? Mika told me.

奥さんは中国の方なんですか？ 日本人だと思ってました。
Okusan wa chūgoku no kata nan desu ka? Nihonjin da to omottemashita.
Is your wife Chinese? I thought she was Japanese.

これ、ベルギーのチョコなんですよ。食べてみてください。
Kore, Berugī no choko nan desu yo. Tabete mite kudasai.
This is Belgian chocolate. Please try some.

わあ、ベルギーに行ったんですか？
Wā, Berugī ni itta n desu ka?
Wow, did you go to Belgium?

いえいえ、お隣さんにもらったんですよ。
Ieie, o-tonari-san ni moratta n desu yo.
No, my neighbor gave them to me.

Forming Longer Sentences

You've probably already reached the point where you'd like to construct longer, more complex sentences in Japanese. To do so, you will need to use modifying clauses. Below are some important tips to keep in mind when building sentences.

Modifying clauses come before the nouns they modify.

noun	modifying clause	
The restaurant	I went to yesterday	was good.

昨日行った	レストラン	はおいしかったです。
Kinou itta	resutoran	wa oishikatta desu.

Any tense can be used for the verb in the modifying clause.

The movie I'm watching now is very interesting.

今みている	映画	はとても面白いです。
Ima mite iru	eiga	wa totemo omoshiroi desu.

Japanese doesn't use relative pronouns (*who, where, which*) with modifying clauses—just attach the clause directly to the noun it modifies.

I know a girl who can speak Japanese.

日本語が話せる	女の子	を知ってます。
Nihongo ga hanseru	onnanoko	o shittemasu.

I like people who are good at drawing.

絵が上手な 人が好きです。

E ga jōzu na hito ga suki desu.

Other modifying words (like i-adjectives) can appear between the noun and its modifying clause.

Do you know a good place where we can talk at?

話ができる いい 場所を知ってますか？

Hanashi ga dekiru ii basho o shittemasu ka?

If a single noun has multiple modifying clauses, separating them with a comma will make it easier for the reader to correctly interpret them.

The movie I saw yesterday starring a cute boy was good.

昨日見た 、かわいい男の子が出ていた 映画はよかった。

Kinou mita, kawaii otokonoko ga deteita eiga wa yokatta.

Clauses can modify any noun in a sentence, including subjects, objects, and other parts of the sentence.

This is the book I was looking for.

これが 私が探していた 本です。

Kore ga watashi ga sagashite ita hon desu.

Counters

small objects (つ is used for ordering food and as a generic counter)		people	small animals (except birds)	long, slender objects (sticks, bottles, etc.)	drinks	flat, thin objects (sheets, tickets, etc.)	machines (cars, mobile phones, etc.)
何個？	いくつ？	何人？	何匹？	何本？	何杯？	何枚？	何台？
1個 ikko	1つ hitotsu	1人 hitori	1匹 ippiki	1本 ippon	1杯 ippai	1枚 ichimai	1台 ichidai
2個 niko	2つ futatsu	2人 futari	2匹 nihiki	2本 nihon	2杯 nihai	2枚 nimai	2台 nidai
3個 sanko	3つ mittsu	3人 sannin	3匹 sanbiki	3本 sanbon	3杯 sanbai	3枚 sanmai	3台 sandai
4個 yonko	4つ yottsu	4人 yonin	4匹 yonhiki	4本 yonhon	4杯 yonhai	4枚 yonmai	4台 yondai
5個 goko	5つ itsutsu	5人 gonin	5匹 gohiki	5本 gohon	5杯 gohai	5枚 gomai	5台 godai
6個 rokko	6つ muttsu	6人 rokunin	6匹 roppiki	6本 roppon	6杯 roppai	6枚 rokumai	6台 rokudai
7個 nanako	7つ nanatsu	7人 nananin	7匹 nanahiki	7本 nanahon	7杯 nanahai	7枚 nanamai	7台 nanadai
8個 hachiko	8つ yattsu	8人 hachinin	8匹 happiki	8本 happon	8杯 happai	8枚 hachimai	8台 hachidai
9個 kyūko	9つ kokonotsu	9人 kyūnin	9匹 kyūhiki	9本 kyūhon	9杯 kyūhai	9枚 kyūmai	9台 kyūdai
10個 jukko	10 tō	10人 jūnin	10匹 juppiki	10本 juppon	10杯 juppai	10枚 jūmai	10台 jūdai

- Counters for one, six, eight, and ten things use a P sound while those for three things use a B sound.
- Other common counters include those for books (冊 or *satsu*), products (点 or *ten*), and stories of a building (階 or *kai*).
- The number 10 is an exception — it doesn't contain つ.

Frequency

一日 ichinichi	に（　） ni	回／度 times / kai
一週間 isshūkan		時間 jikan
一ヵ月 ikkagetsu		日 ka / nichi
一年 ichinen		

週に１回
shū ni ikkai
one time per week

月に４回
tsuki ni yon-kai
four times per month

一日に何回ご飯を食べますか？
Ichinichi ni nankai gohan o tabemasu ka?
How many times do you eat per day?

一日に３回ご飯を食べます。
Ichinichi ni san-kai gohan o tabemasu. *I eat three times each day.*

一週間に 40 時間働いています。
Isshūkan ni yonjū-jikan hataraite imasu. *I work 40 hours a week.*

一ヵ月に２日、学校があります。
Ikkagetsu ni futsuka gakkō ga arimasu. *We have school two days a month.*

● Sometimes the number before the counter is dropped if it is 1:

年に一度、祭りがある。
Nen ni ichido, matsuri ga aru. *There's a festival once a year.*

● You can also add a number other than 1 to indicate a different frequency:

２日に一度、洗濯します。
Futsuka ni ichido, sentaku shimasu.
I do laundry once every two days.

３ヵ月に一回、実家に帰ります。
Sankagetsu ni ikkai, jikka ni kaerimasu.
I return to my parents' house once every three months.

Transitive and Intransitive Verbs

subject は object を transitive verb		subject が intransitive verb	
開《あ》ける to open	ドアを開《あ》けてください。 Please open the door.	開《あ》く to open	店《みせ》が開《あ》いています。 The store is open.
閉《し》める to close	ドアを閉《し》めてください。 Please close the door.	閉《し》まる to close	店が閉《し》まっています。 The store is closed.
つける to turn on	電気《でんき》をつけましょうか。 Shall I turn on the light?	つく to be on	電気《でんき》がついています。 The light is on.
消《け》す to turn off	電気《でんき》を消《け》してもいいですか。 Can I turn off the light?	消《き》える to be off	消《き》えています。 The light is off.
止《と》める to stop	車《くるま》を止《と》めてください。 Please stop the car.	止《と》まる to stop	車《くるま》が止《と》まっています。 The car is stopped.
落《お》とす to drop	カギを落《お》としました。 I dropped my key.	落《お》ちる to fall	葉《は》っぱが落《お》ちていました。 The leaves had fallen.
割《わ》る to break	コップを割《わ》って しまいました。 I accidentally broke the cup.	割《わ》れる to break	ガラスが割《わ》れています。 The glass is broken.
変《か》える to change	予定《よてい》を変《か》えました。 I changed my plans.	変《か》わる to change	天気《てんき》が変《か》わりました。 The weather changed.
決《き》める to decide	目標《もくひょう》を決《き》めました。 I decided on my goal.	決《き》まる to be decided	スケジュールが 決《き》まりました。 The schedule has been decided.
出《だ》す to take out to submit	宿題《しゅくだい》を出《だ》してください。 Hand in your homework.	出《で》る to go out to leave	会社《かいしゃ》から出《で》たところです。 I just left the office.
倒《たお》す to knock over	敵《てき》を倒《たお》した。 I knocked over my enemy.	倒《たお》れる to fall over	地震《じしん》でビルが倒《たお》れました。 The earthquake toppled the building.

When in Japan, you might see a stop sign that says 止まれ. This is the command form of とまる, an intransitive verb. Unlike transitive verbs, which are used when the action affects an object (someone or something), intransitive verbs do not have an object. In English, some verbs can be both transitive or intransitive depending on how they are used in a sentence. Japanese often uses pairs of verbs that differ slightly to make this distinction.

Practical Japanese 2

2018年 10月 7日　第1刷発行

著　者 小川 清美

発行者 浦　晋亮

発行所 IBCパブリッシング株式会社
〒162-0804 東京都新宿区中里町29番3号 菱秀神楽坂ビル9F
Tel. 03-3513-4511 Fax. 03-3513-4512
www.ibcpub.co.jp

印刷所 株式会社シナノパブリッシングプレス

ISBN978-4-7946-0561-0